TOXIC RELATIONSHIPS

A BIBLICAL GUIDE AND REFLECTIVE JOURNAL TO HELP YOU IDENTIFY, CONFRONT, AND BREAK THE CYCLE OF TOXICITY IN ROMANCE, FAMILY, FRIENDSHIPS, AND WORK

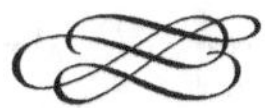

MARY MELISSA HALL

CONTENTS

For my Lord and Savior Jesus Christ. In Him, I live and move and have my being (Acts 17:28). He is my Reason for being and the Source of every good thing in my life.

Andy, thank you for being my perfect dream man and for not being toxic! Isaiah, Shiloh, and Zion, thank you for being so excited about my new endeavor. I love all of you more than words could ever express. I'm so thankful God gave me you!

Do you want to breathe new life into your relationships?

Scan the QR code to get 10 life-changing **Relationship Affirmations and Scriptures** delivered to your inbox for FREE!

INTRODUCTION

INTRODUCTION

Have you ever felt misunderstood, taken for granted, or resented? Do you know the sting of being vilified for unintentionally saying or doing something that offended someone else? Have you ever felt like you had to tiptoe around certain people, your breath catching in your throat over mere trivialities that shouldn't cause such fear? Do you sometimes feel invisible--or worse, despised-- just for being yourself? Many of us have lived through these painful experiences for years, wondering what we did wrong and how we could be forgiven for whatever we did that no one would tell us. You might have faced moments that made you question, "Is this how relationships are supposed to be?"

This book was born out of a deep desire to address these silent battles many people endure. I've been there—feeling trapped in a cycle of emotional turmoil, wondering if I was the problem. Through personal struggles and years of supporting others, I've learned essential truths I want to share. This isn't just a book; it's a journey we'll take together to identify, confront, and break the cycle of toxic relationships across all areas of life: romance, family, friendships, and work.

Before we proceed, I want to make clear that this book is *not* about abuse of any kind: physical, emotional, verbal, mental, etc. It's crucial to acknowledge that if you or your family members are in danger or experiencing abuse in any form, please seek professional help immediately. The issues discussed in this book are serious and worthy of our time and attention, but they do not refer to abuse, which is much deeper and requires much more support than this book offers.

As we will learn throughout the book, there is a spectrum of toxicity. Abusive relationships are most definitely toxic, but on the other end of the toxicity spectrum are relationships that are draining and unhealthy. They chip away at your self-esteem and happiness, but they are not necessarily abusive. This book addresses these types of toxic relationships. For example, you may have a grumpy family member, a jealous sister, a nagging mother, or a gossiping, competitive coworker. You may not desire to end these relationships completely, or perhaps you can't, but you are just wondering if these individuals are toxic and if you can do anything about it.

We'll explore four key areas where toxicity can seep in, providing you with tools to identify, confront, and ultimately break free from these harmful patterns. Each section includes reflection questions, related Bible verses, affirmations to speak aloud, and action items to guide your path to recovery and empowerment.

Why am I so passionate about this topic? Because I've lived it. I've felt the sting of harsh words, the isolation of manipulation, and the guilt that comes from believing I was at fault. But I discovered that healing was possible through faith in Jesus Christ and His Word. This book blends Biblical wisdom with psychological insights, offering a balanced perspective that nurtures your spiritual and emotional well-being.

Journaling and self-reflection are core components of this guide. They're tools that allow you to dig deep and process your learning. I suggest grabbing a notebook and pen and answering the reflection questions at the end of each chapter. Or, if you have the book's printed version, write directly on the pages. Something magically freeing happens when you get your thoughts out of your head and onto paper. As you write down your ideas and complete the action items, you're not just reading a book—you're engaging in a conversation with yourself about what you truly need and deserve. Additionally, it is a great idea to speak aloud the related Scriptures and affirmations at the end of each chapter. The more you hear your own voice declaring freedom and positive change over your life, the more your brain starts to believe it.

Remember, this journey is about empowerment. You are not at fault for the toxicity you've experienced, nor are you alone in this struggle. You can break free from these cycles and enjoy a life filled with peace and happiness. This book is here to remind you of your strength and resilience, to offer hope, and to guide you toward that freedom.

So, let's step forward together. Open this book with an open heart, ready to face the truths within these pages, and embrace the transformation that awaits. Here's to finding peace, reclaiming joy, and building healthier relationships. Welcome to a new chapter in your life!

CHAPTER 1

THE FOUNDATION OF TOXIC RELATIONSHIPS

So, let's talk about something that, unfortunately, too many of us are all too familiar with—those relationships that leave us feeling less like ourselves and more like extras in a lousy movie. You know, the kind where you might think, "Did that really just happen?" more often than not. It's like living in a loop of your least favorite drama series, but you can't find the remote to change the channel. Well, it's time to find that remote!

Toxic relationships can sneak into our lives, whether we're talking about romantic entanglements, family feuds, not-so-friendly friends, or even those dread-inducing workplace dramas. But what does 'toxic' really mean? It's a buzzword that gets thrown around a lot, but it's crucial to unpack it and understand the mechanics before we can kick it to the curb. So buckle up, my friend, because we're about to take a deep dive into the psychology of toxic relationships. We'll explore the behaviors that poison our interactions and how these can profoundly affect our minds and spirits. And yes, we'll also check what God's Word says about all this mess!

. . .

Decoding the Psychology of Toxicity

Understanding the layers of toxic relationships is like being a detective in a psychological thriller. You might not be wearing a trench coat and interviewing shady characters in dimly lit rooms, but you're piecing together clues about behaviors and patterns that can seriously mess with your peace of mind.

First off, toxicity in relationships isn't just about narcissism, though that's a biggie. It's about a range of behaviors that quietly chip away at your well-being through conflict, competition, and control. A toxic relationship is one in which unhealthy communication is used by one or both people. This can lead to a whole slew of additional toxic behaviors, which we are going to dive into throughout the book.

As stated in the introduction, there is a spectrum of toxicity, and it is often hard to decipher where your relationships fall on this scale. I will tread very lightly here, because I know it is a painful subject. No one but you fully knows the extent of what you have experienced, so it will take careful discernment on your part to determine if your relationships could be toxic.

Abusive relationships are definitely toxic, but not all toxic relationships are abusive. This book is about examining relationships that are toxic to the point of eroding your self-esteem, happiness, and well-being but are not necessarily abusive. However, there is often a fine line between toxic behaviors that are non-abusive and those that are abusive. Only you know the full scope of your personal situation. If you feel the toxic treatment you are experiencing could actually be abuse of some kind (mental, emotional, psychological, etc.), please seek help as soon as possible from a qualified professional. You have great value in God's eyes and deserve healthy relationships.

Imagine a family member constantly denying things you both know are true, making you question your reality. This, my dear reader, is called gaslighting, and it's often present in toxic relationships. It's a form of psychological manipulation where, over time, you start to doubt your memory and perception. Think of it as psychological warfare where the weapon is doubt, and it's pointed right at your sanity.

But wait, there's more! Other toxic manipulation tactics include the use of guilt, shame, or fear. Picture a friend who makes you feel guilty every time you can't meet up or a boss who shames you in front of colleagues to keep you in line. These tactics can seriously erode your self-esteem and self-worth, making you constantly afraid of doing something wrong.

Now, who are the usual suspects in these scenarios? Often, they're individuals who may themselves be wrestling with untreated mental health issues or who have learned these behaviors as a way to cope with their insecurities. It's not an excuse for their behavior, but it helps to understand the 'why' behind the 'what.'

The impact on you, the victim, can be profound. Constant exposure to toxic behaviors can lead to anxiety, depression, and a plummet in self-esteem. You might feel constantly on edge, sad, or hopeless about your relationship dynamics.

From a Biblical perspective, such toxicity starkly contrasts teachings on love, respect, and kindness. Scriptures teach us that love is patient and kind and keeps no record of wrongs—pretty much the opposite of what happens in toxic relationships. Reflecting on these Biblical truths, it becomes clear that these toxic behaviors have no place in our lives.

Understanding these dynamics is the first step towards cleaning house in your relational world. It's about recognizing the signs, understanding the sources, and starting to say "no more" to the drama. And remember, my friend, this isn't about pointing fingers or assigning blame. It's about empowering you to recognize unhealthy patterns and start crafting healthier, happier relationships that uplift, not undermine. So, let's keep turning those pages and find out how to switch off that bad drama once and for all!

Biblical Perspectives on Healthy vs. Unhealthy Relationships

Navigating relationships can sometimes feel like deciphering a complicated recipe without any measurements—exciting, yes, but also a bit baffling. Wouldn't it be wonderful if there was a simple, straightforward guide to help us distinguish the nourishing from the toxic? Well, guess what? There is! God's Word, the Bible, can be your go-to resource for understanding the essentials of healthy relationships.

Let's start with what the Scriptures say about how we should treat each other. It goes way beyond just being nice. The Bible paints a picture of relationships built on love, respect, and mutual edification. It's not just about avoiding conflict or smiling through gritted teeth; it's about actively seeking the best for each other. Think about the kind of love described in 1 Corinthians 13—patient, kind, not envious or boastful. It's the kind of love that doesn't keep a score of wrongs (and let's be honest, who doesn't want to throw away that notepad sometimes?).

But here's where it gets real: love in the Bible isn't just a fluffy feeling; it's actionable. It's love that rolls up its sleeves and gets down to business. It's about making choices that prioritize another's well-being, even when inconvenient. Imagine a scenario where a friend is moving, and it's the big game night. Showing love might mean you record the game for later viewing and help them haul boxes instead. It's that proactive kind of love that sees a need and responds.

Now, let's chat about God's model of love. It's the gold standard. God's love for us is unconditional, not based on what we do or how well we perform. God loved us so much that He sent His Son, Jesus, to die for our sins and give us everlasting life. If you have never received this divine Truth and asked Jesus to be your Lord and Savior, now is the perfect time to do so! It will cause this book to make much more sense. You can speak a simple prayer from your heart, such as, "Lord Jesus, I believe you died on the cross for my sins and rose again. Please come into my heart and be my Savior and Lord." It's that easy!

This divine love is our benchmark in all relationships. It teaches us to extend grace and love unconditionally, which can be challenging, especially when we're wired to think in terms of 'give and take.' Yet, embracing this concept can radically transform our interactions, making our relationships more about giving freely and less about keeping tabs.

Let's put this Biblical love into action in our everyday lives. It can be as simple as listening—really listening—to someone share about their day without glancing at your phone or crafting your response before they've even finished speaking. It could also be showing empathy when someone is upset, even if you don't fully understand why they're hurt. Each day gives us countless opportunities to demonstrate love through small, meaningful actions. These consistent acts of love and respect build a sturdy, healthy relationship that can weather tough times.

Reflecting on these principles makes it clear just how contrasting toxic behaviors are to the teachings of the Bible. Where toxicity undermines and devalues, Biblical love uplifts and restores. This doesn't just happen by chance; it requires a conscious decision to filter our actions and reactions through the truth of what love is. This isn't about becoming a doormat; it's about becoming a doorway to a new kind of relationship that mirrors the love, respect, and kindness God shows us.

As we consider these Scriptural truths, let's challenge ourselves to embody this love! Let's make it real in the checkout line, boardroom, or at the dinner table and transform our little corners of the world one act of genuine love at a time.

. . .

Respect and Honor in Relationships: A Biblical Mandate

Now, let's look at the foundation of every rock-solid relationship: respect. It's like the concrete base of a skyscraper—it doesn't matter how beautiful the penthouse suite is; if the foundation isn't solid, things will crumble sooner rather than later. Ephesians 5:33 gives us a clear directive: Each one of you must love his wife as he loves himself, and the wife must respect her husband. But this isn't just about marital bliss; it's a universal principle that applies to all relationships. Respect is the underpinning of genuine connection and trust. Without it, well, you're building on sand. (See the parable about the wise and foolish builders in Matthew 7:24-27).

Now, let's unpack the power of words because, as Proverbs 18:21 tells us, the tongue has the power of life and death. Words can be the wings on which our relationships soar or the weights that drag them down. Think about it: How often do careless words cause a rift in a friendship? Or how often has a thoughtlessly sharp remark soured a family gathering? On the flip side, consider when a timely, kind word has lifted your spirits or healed a breach. Words aren't just sounds passed between us; they're carriers of life. They have the power to build up or tear down, to start wars, or pave the way for peace. God Himself used words to speak the universe into existence.

In the dance of relationships, mutual submission plays a pivotal role. Ephesians 5:21 urges us to submit to one another out of reverence for Christ. This isn't about losing your voice or becoming less than; it's about fostering a culture of mutual respect and support. It's a call to value the other's needs and perspectives as highly as yours. Imagine a scenario where a husband and wife are deciding how to spend a mutual day off. Mutual submission looks like each person genuinely considering the other's ideas and desires before making a decision together. It's a beautiful, reciprocal act of honoring each other and is as far from being a doormat as the East is from the West.

Speaking of respect, it's crucial even when we disagree. Disagreements are inevitable, but they don't have to be destructive. It's all about the approach. Instead of entering a discussion with guns blazing, we can choose to keep our words respectful and our tone even. It's like deciding to pass the salt rather than throw it. When you approach disagreements with respect, you keep the doors of communication open, and you stand a much better chance of reaching a solution that respects both parties' views.

Boundaries are another key aspect of healthy relationships, and yes, they're totally Biblical. Jesus Himself set boundaries. He took time for solitude away from the crowds. He knew when to say yes and how to say no. Setting boundaries is about loving ourselves and others well. It's not selfish; it's necessary for healthy interaction. For instance, saying no to a friend who wants to monopolize every Friday night doesn't mean you don't value the friendship; it means you value your other relationships and commitments just as much.

Finally, let's touch on forgiveness versus reconciliation. Forgiveness is required of us as believers in Christ; it's about letting go of bitterness and choosing peace. It doesn't excuse the behavior of the person who hurt you; it sets *you* free. You don't have to *feel* like forgiving in order to do so.

Consider the following strategy I learned from a mentor. When someone hurts her feelings, she says, "I forgive this person, Lord, as you have forgiven me," even though she doesn't feel like she has forgiven at all! She still feels deeply hurt and resentful. However, as she continually repeats this phrase whenever thoughts of the person come into her mind, slowly, little by little, the feeling of forgiveness eventually comes. I can tell you from experience that this strategy works. After all, God has forgiven us of so much. How can we not forgive others?

On the other hand, reconciliation is a different ball game. Reconciliation is about the complete restoration of the relationship. This should be conditional, based on the readiness and safety of the situation. You can forgive someone without restoring the relationship to what it was before. Forgiveness frees your heart, but wisdom dictates the future of the relationship. Just because you forgive someone doesn't mean you have to be around them all the time (unless, of course, you live with them, which is a whole other topic).

Navigating these dynamics with grace and wisdom strengthens our relationships and aligns them more closely with how God intends us to relate to one another. In a world that often models relationships based on power or tit-for-tat, adopting a Biblical approach to respect and honor is not just countercultural; it's transformative. It's about building relationships that are not only enduring but also leave a legacy of love and respect that reflects the heart of God. As we model this in our lives, we become beacons of light in our relationships, whether at home, among friends, or within our wider communities.

The Spectrum of Toxicity: Identifying Subtle Signs

When we think about toxic relationships, it's easy to imagine the big, dramatic blowouts you see in movies, where dishes are thrown and doors are slammed. But in reality, the signs are often much less noticeable and start as small, almost imperceptible behaviors that slowly seep into our daily interactions like a slow-dripping faucet you hardly notice—until the sink overflows. Understanding these subtle beginnings is like becoming a relationship detective, where you learn to spot the clues before they turn into a full-blown mystery with no happy ending.

Now, let's talk about the red flags that aren't as clear as a stop sign. Imagine you're in a new relationship, and everything seems peachy. But slowly, you notice your partner making jokes about your career choices at dinner parties, disguising them as "just teasing." Or perhaps your friend consistently "forgets" their wallet every time you meet for coffee, leaving you to cover the bill again. These behaviors might seem minor at first glance, but they can be early indicators of disrespect and manipulation, which are cornerstone traits of a toxic relationship. Another less obvious red flag is inconsistency in communication, where you receive affection in abundance one day and then silence the next—leaving you wondering what you did wrong.

Awareness and acknowledgment of these signs are crucial in preventing deeper entanglement, which can lead to more severe emotional and psychological consequences. It's about catching the small leaks before they become floods. Being vigilant can help you address issues early on or decide when it might be time to step back from a relationship that's showing signs of becoming toxic.

Let's look at some real-life scenarios. Consider Jen, a friend of mine, who noticed that her boyfriend often insisted on choosing movies and dinner spots, subtly dismissing her preferences each time. Initially, she thought he was just being assertive and taking charge, a trait she admired. However, as she became more aware of this pattern, she realized it was a control tactic, not assertiveness. By recognizing these subtle signs, Jen addressed the issue early on, which led to conversations about respect and decision-making in the relationship.

Another example is my former coworker Michael, who noticed another coworker was often dismissive of his career achievements. This initially seemed like insecurity on the coworker's part, but Michael soon recognized it as a pattern of undermining behavior that left him feeling undervalued. In both cases, early recognition allowed them to address the behaviors directly or make informed decisions about the future of these relationships.

In these stories and countless others, the key takeaway is the power of tuning into the subtleties of how we are treated in our relationships. Often, it's not the grand gestures but the small, everyday interactions that shape the health and happiness of our relational dynamics. By staying alert to these subtle signs, we empower ourselves to cultivate truly nurturing relationships and avoid those that drain our spirits. So, as you navigate your interactions, keep your eyes open for the small things—they're often telling you more than you might think.

Empowerment Through Awareness: Your First Step to Freedom

Let's face it: realizing you're in a toxic relationship can feel like waking up to find your GPS has been navigating you in circles. It's disorienting and frustrating; you want to find the exit route to somewhere sunny and calm. The good news? Knowledge is your new best friend, and it's about giving you the power to drive your life in a new direction. Understanding the dynamics of toxic relationships is like turning on the floodlights at a nighttime soccer game; suddenly, you can see the whole field, and you're not just kicking at shadows anymore.

So, how do you start this process? Begin with a bit of reflection and self-assessment. It's like checking the weather before you plan a picnic. Will it be sunny skies with your circle of friends, or are storm clouds gathering on the horizon? Proverbs, with its timeless wisdom, encourages us to seek out uplifting and honest relationships. So, ask yourself: Do my relationships feel uplifting? Do they bring peace and joy into my life, or is there a constant undercurrent of stress and discomfort?

Now, if you're seeing more storm clouds than sunshine, it might be time for some actionable steps. First things first, set some boundaries. This doesn't mean building a fortress around your heart, but rather, it's like setting up a nice, respectful fence. Boundaries communicate to others how you expect to be treated—kind of like how traffic lights direct traffic. If someone keeps running the red light, it's probably time to reroute that relationship.

Another practical step? Have honest conversations. Yes, it can be challenging, but think of it as pulling out the weeds so your garden can thrive. Approach these talks with a spirit of love and clarity. Explain how certain behaviors make you feel and what changes you want to see. Remember, it's not about confrontation; it's about construction—building healthier, happier relationship dynamics. I would definitely suggest praying for a while before taking this step, and remember, timing is everything. So, try to initiate the conversation when the other person seems in a good mood and is open to honesty. Also, be prepared to take a break or leave the relationship if the other person does not respond favorably.

Finally, here is where the encouragement and hope come in. You are not alone in this situation. Countless others have navigated this path before you, finding their way out of the fog and into healthier relationships. Lean on these shared experiences and draw strength from them. Moreover, the Bible is packed with promises of strength, renewal, and hope. Verses like Isaiah 40:31 remind us that those who hope in the Lord will renew their strength. They will soar on wings like eagles; they will run and not grow weary; they will walk and not be faint.

Embrace these truths. Let them be the catalysts for positive change in your relationships. Remember, every step you take toward understanding and addressing toxicity in your relationships is a step toward freedom. It's a step toward a life where peace, joy, and love aren't just occasional visitors but permanent residents in your heart and home.

So, take these insights off the page and into your life. Reflect, assess, act, and transform. The road ahead is bright, leading to places filled with hope and healing. With every step of empowerment through awareness, you're not just surviving but thriving. And as you continue to grow and navigate through these experiences, remember that with each moment of courage, each day you choose health and happiness over toxicity, you are reshaping not only your life but also setting the stage for stronger, more fulfilling relationships that reflect the true beauty of who you are.

Reflection Questions:

Who do I need to forgive?

Could my relationship with this person be toxic?

Can I talk to this person about the issue(s) that bother(s) me?

What boundaries do I need to set in this relationship?

Related Scriptures:

In Him we have redemption (deliverance and salvation) through His blood, the remission (forgiveness) of our offenses (shortcomings and trespasses), in accordance with the riches *and* the generosity of His gracious favor (Ephesians 1:7, AMPC).

A friend loves at all times, and is born, as is a brother, for adversity (Proverbs 17:17, AMPC).

Affirmations to Speak Aloud:

In the Name of Jesus, I declare:

- God loves me.
- I am worthy to be loved.
- I love people with the love of Christ.
- I forgive freely.
- I forgive ___________ because You, Lord, have forgiven me.

* * *

Action Item(s):

Grab a journal and pen and create two columns. In the first column, jot down the names of people you spend the most time with. Next to each name, in the second column, write how you feel after you've spent time with them. Are you energized or drained? Valued or diminished? This isn't about making snap judgments; it's about starting to notice patterns. Reflect on your findings and decide if there is anyone with whom you may need to set some boundaries.

CHAPTER 2

THE IMPACT OF TOXIC RELATIONSHIPS

Have you ever noticed how a really stressful day can leave you feeling like you've just run a marathon, complete with sore muscles and exhaustion? Or how, after a heated argument, you might find yourself nursing a headache or feeling utterly spent? It turns out the drama of toxic relationships can similarly take a toll on your body. It's like your body is the stage for a Shakespearean tragedy, where the stress is the lead actor, wreaking havoc scene after scene. Let's dive into how these relationships can push our bodies to the brink and what we can do about it.

The Physical Toll: A Body Under Siege

So, how exactly does a toxic relationship send your body into a tizzy? Imagine your body as a well-oiled machine—everything's running smoothly, gears are turning, and then suddenly, stress enters the scene like sand in the gears. This stress isn't just a fleeting guest; in toxic relationships, it's a regular visitor who doesn't know when to leave. The constant pressure and emotional turmoil act like a continual stress response in your body. This can lead to a whole host of health issues, from headaches and fatigue to more serious problems like high blood pressure and heart disease. Yes, your heart can literally ache from toxic relationships!

Now, recognizing the signs that your body is under siege can be complicated. It's not like your body sends out a formal announcement: "Alert: we are under stress! Please adjust accordingly!" Instead, it gives you hints. Maybe it's that constant tension you feel in your shoulders, the stomach upsets that occur more frequently, or perhaps it's the insomnia that keeps you awake at night, replaying those arguments in your head. These symptoms are your body's way of waving a red flag, signaling that the drama is more than just an emotional burden—it's a physical one, too.

So, what can you do to protect your castle from this siege? First, let's talk about self-care. And no, self-care isn't just bubble baths and chocolate cake—although those things are certainly nice! Biblical self-care involves honoring the temple God has given you by taking proactive steps to maintain your spiritual, mental, and physical health (spirit, soul, and body). This means setting aside time, perhaps at the start of each day, to connect with God through prayer and reading His Word. This simple practice helps center your thoughts, calm your spirit, and get your day started on a positive note. Physical exercise is also crucial; it's like telling the stress, "You're not going to keep me down!" Even something as simple as a daily walk can boost your mood and improve your health.

But sometimes, self-care and lifestyle changes might not be enough. It's important to recognize when you need to call in the reinforcements. Seeking professional help, be it medical advice for those stress-related ailments or counseling to navigate the emotional minefields, is not a sign of weakness—it's a strategic move towards strength. Remember, like Esther's story, seeking wise counsel is pivotal in overcoming challenges.

. . .

Stress Symptom Checklist

Here's a simple checklist to help you track how your body might react to relationship stress. Check off (or make a note of) any symptoms you've experienced recently:

- Headaches
- Muscle tension or pain
- Fatigue
- Stomach upset
- Sleep disturbances
- Anxiety
- Feelings of sadness
- Inability to concentrate
- Low self-esteem
- Poor self-image

This checklist isn't just to monitor symptoms; it's a tool to prompt you into action. If you're checking off multiple items, it might be time to consider what steps you can take to reduce stress and improve your well-being. Whether it's adjusting your boundaries in the relationship, enhancing your self-care routine, or seeking professional help, remember that you are worth the effort. Your health is a precious gift, and maintaining it isn't just about feeling good—it's about honoring the life God has given you.

In this chapter, as we dissect the physical repercussions of toxic relationships, remember the goal is not to foster fear or create an inventory of complaints but to empower you to change your circumstances. It's about recognizing the signs, taking charge of your health, and making informed decisions that lead to a happier, healthier you. So, as you turn these pages, think of each word as a stepping stone away from stress and toward peace. Your body—

and your heart—will thank you for it.

Emotional Scars: The Heart's Wounds

Oh, the heart! It's not just a biological marvel pumping life through our veins—it's also where we feel the most profound joys and, unfortunately, the deepest hurts. When it comes to toxic relationships, the heart takes a frontline hit. It's like carrying around a little internal echo of every harsh word or cold shoulder you've ever received. These aren't just fleeting stings; they're wounds that can leave lasting scars on your emotional well-being. But despite the deep cuts, the beauty of the heart lies in its remarkable ability to heal and grow stronger, especially when given the proper care.

Let's first understand the emotional impact of these toxic entanglements. Imagine your emotions as a garden. In a healthy relationship, this garden is filled with love, yielding joy, peace, and fulfillment. In contrast, a toxic relationship tramples this garden underfoot, leaving weeds of doubt, insecurity, and fear that choke out all life and color. It's not just about feeling sad or upset; it's a deeper erosion of your emotional landscape, where you might question your worth or lose sight of your feelings and needs. It's like you're constantly wearing gray-tinted glasses, and everything that was once bright has dulled.

Recognizing this emotional distress can be tricky because it often creeps up silently. It might start with feeling uneasy or anxious without knowing why. Maybe you're quicker to tears, or you find yourself withdrawing from things you used to love, like catching the latest movie or just laughing over coffee with friends. These signs are your body's way of waving a red flag, trying to get your attention that something is off.

Now, how do you start healing these emotional scars? It's a process, not an overnight fix, involving a combination of spiritual nourishment and psychological strategies. One of the first steps is to reclaim your emotional space. This means giving yourself permission to feel your feelings without judgment. Expressing what you're going through can be incredibly therapeutic—whether it's through talking to a trusted friend, journaling, or even creative outlets like painting or music. It's about externalizing those tangled emotions so they don't stay cooped up, festering inside. When we take an honest look at what's happening, we can start to address and resolve it.

Scripturally, we can find immense comfort knowing we are not alone in our sufferings. The Psalms, for example, are filled with heartfelt cries and lamentations, reminding us that expressing our deepest sorrows is a part of the human experience and nothing to be ashamed of. Psalm 34:18 says, "The Lord is close to the broken-hearted and saves those who are crushed in spirit." These words can be a soothing balm, reassuring that your pain is seen and you are not forgotten.

Pairing these spiritual encouragements with psychological techniques can also enhance your healing journey. Cognitive-behavioral strategies, for instance, help identify and challenge the negative thought patterns that toxic relationships often imprint on us. It's about rewiring those automatic thoughts of "I'm not good enough" or "I don't deserve better" and replacing them with truths about your inherent worth in Christ. You are worth so much to Father God that He gave His Son to die for you. Your worth is far above rubies (Proverbs 31:10).

Rebuilding emotional health is akin to nurturing that trampled garden back to life. It involves intentional reliance on Christ, self-growth, establishing healthy boundaries, and slowly but surely allowing yourself to trust and open up again. It's also about resilience. Just as a garden adapts to the changing seasons, you can adjust and grow through the experiences you've endured. This doesn't mean the scars magically disappear but become less defining of your life's story. Instead, they are testaments to your strength and your capacity to renew yourself despite the odds.

Remember, healing doesn't return to where you were but grows into where you want to be. It's a forward motion transforming into a life where your emotional well-being is treasured and protected. So, take it one day at a time, one step at a time, knowing that each step is a victory and a rebellion against the toxicity that once tried to define you. You are more than your past hurts, more resilient than ever imagined, and capable of cultivating an emotional landscape rich with love, peace, and joy.

Spiritual Struggles: Maintaining Faith Amidst Toxicity

Navigating through a toxic relationship can sometimes feel like trying to find your way through a thick fog with a flickering light. It's disorienting, and frankly, it can make you question your compass—your faith. When every day tosses a new challenge your way, it's not just the mind and body that feel the weight; your spirit does, too. It's like you're in a tiny boat rocked by wave after wave, and holding on to your faith feels like trying to clutch a slippery fish! But here's the thing—your faith isn't just another item in your emotional toolkit; it's the anchor that can keep you steady, even in stormy seas.

Let's unpack this a bit, shall we? When you're caught in the whirlwind of a toxic relationship, it can start to cloud your spiritual vision. You might wonder why, if you've been faithful in your walk with Christ, you've wound up in such a troubling situation. It's a bit like Job, feeling besieged by trials on every side, questioning the fairness of it all. This questioning is perfectly natural, but it also creates an opportunity for growth—a chance to dig deeper into your beliefs and the nature of your spiritual resilience. It's about turning the 'Why is this happening?' into 'How can my faith bring me through this?'

Strengthening your faith in these trying times can seem daunting, but it's absolutely possible and starts with getting back to basics. Dive into the Word of God like it is a love letter written just for you at this moment in your life. Scriptures that reaffirm God's presence and promises can be a balm for your weary heart. Consider David in the Psalms—his raw, unfiltered conversations with God aren't just ancient texts; they demonstrate how to wrestle with and yet hold on to faith when the going gets tough.

However, strengthening your faith doesn't have to be a solo journey. This is where the beauty of your spiritual community comes into play. Whether it's a church family, a small Bible study group, or even online forums, these networks can offer incredible support and affirmation. They remind you that you're not trekking through this toxic wasteland alone. There's power in gathering, even virtually, to share your burdens and find collective strength. Just as Moses needed Aaron and Hur to hold up his arms during battle, sometimes we need our spiritual squad to hold us up when our strength wanes.

Now, let's talk about God's role in all this. It's easy to blame God for anything unpleasant in our lives. However, the truth is that God doesn't send bad things to us, and He is more than willing to bring us through them. His promise to never leave nor forsake us isn't just a fair-weather pledge; it's an all-season commitment. Recognizing God's presence in your struggle can shift your perspective tremendously. It's about seeing your situation not just as a series of unfortunate events but as part of a larger narrative that He is weaving in your life. God's role isn't just to whisk away the challenge (a.k.a. the toxic person); sometimes, it's to strengthen us through it, turning our trials into testimonies and our victimhood into victory.

Embracing this concept can transform the way you view your spiritual journey. It's not about battling to keep your faith intact but deepening it through battle. It's about moving from survival to growth, from questioning to deeper understanding. And as you navigate this path, remember that the same power that raised Christ from the dead is at work within you. That power can renew your spirit and guide you to a place of peace and restoration.

So, keep your faith community close and God's Word closer, always leaving your heart open to what He is speaking to you through Your time spent with Him. God's Word is both the map and the journey to freedom, leading you not just out of toxicity but into greater wholeness.

Social Isolation: Rebuilding Your Support Network

Toxic relationships often come with a side of isolation. It starts subtly; it could be a comment here or there about the time you spend with others or a continuous pattern of conflict before social gatherings that leaves you too drained to attend. Over time, these behaviors can lead to a shrinking social circle and increasing loneliness. It is crucial to realize this isolation is taking place, not just for your emotional health but for your overall recovery and well-being. Signs might include feeling out of touch with friends, a calendar that once brimmed with social engagements now collecting dust, or a sense of dread or guilt at the thought of socializing. These are your clues that it's time to act, reach out, and rebuild those bridges that connect you to others.

Rebuilding your social support network doesn't mean you must dive right back into a whirlwind of social activities. It's about starting small and intentional. Reconnecting can be as simple as texting a friend you haven't contacted in a while or reaching out to a family member to catch up over coffee. It's about planting seeds of reconnection and nurturing them patiently. Remember, it's not about the quantity of interactions but the quality. Look for people who uplift you, provide a listening ear, and remind you of your worth.

The church and Christian community play a pivotal role in this process. These communities are not just gatherings; they are families bound by faith and love, designed to support and uplift each other. Consider joining a small group, attending a worship service, or getting involved in a church project. These activities can provide a sense of belonging and purpose, helping to fill the void left by isolation. Furthermore, these communities are often equipped with resources for emotional and spiritual support, offering counseling, prayer groups, and fellowship activities that can be vital during your healing process.

But what about forming new relationships? After experiencing toxicity, the idea of trusting new people can be daunting. Here, let the principles of Biblical love guide you. Look for relationships embodying patience, kindness, and sincerity that echo Christ's love. Start by engaging in activities that align with your interests and values, whether a Bible study group, a volunteer organization, or a local hobby class. These environments are great for meeting people who may share your interests and values. Remember, building new relationships is a journey. It takes time, discernment, and prayer. It's about finding your tribe—those who share your faith and encourage you to grow. Surrounding yourself with people who support you and genuinely like being around you is essential. As Mike Murdock says, "Go where you're celebrated, not tolerated."

As you work on reconnecting with old friends and forging new bonds, keep in mind that every phone call made, every coffee date set, and every church event attended is a step towards a fuller, more connected life. It's about breaking down those walls that isolation built around you, letting the light back in, and feeling the warmth of community once again. So take that step, send that text, or join that group. Your support network is waiting to welcome you back, and there's a spot just for you, ready to flourish among friends and faith alike.

In wrapping up this chapter on the impact of toxic relationships, we've looked at understanding the physical toll, the emotional scars, the spiritual struggles, and the social isolation these relationships can cause. Each section has highlighted the challenges and provided practical steps and spiritual insights to help you navigate your path to recovery. As you move forward, remember that healing is not just about moving away from something negative but towards something positive—healthier relationships, stronger faith, and a renewed sense of community. With each step, you're not just recovering; you're transforming, growing stronger and more resilient in the light of His love.

As we turn the page to the next chapter, let's carry forward this momentum, this commitment to heal and thrive in every aspect of our lives. With each step, remember that you are surrounded by a community of faith ready to support you along the way.

* * *

Reflection Questions:

Do I feel physically or emotionally drained after being around certain people? If so, who are these people?

How can I limit my exposure to them?

What action steps can I take to grow in my relationship with Jesus (i.e., start my day with prayer, read a chapter in the Bible daily)?

What action steps can I take to grow my relationships with positive, uplifting people (i.e., join a Bible study, ask a friend or family member to meet for coffee)?

* * *

Related Scriptures:

A friend loves at all times, and is born, as is a brother, for adversity (Proverbs 17:17, AMPC).

I can do all things through Christ which strengtheneth me (Philippians 4:13, KJV).

And we know that in all things, God works for the good of those who love Him, who have been called according to his purpose (Romans 8:28, NIV).

Affirmations to Speak Aloud:
In the Name of Jesus, I declare:

- I let go of toxic relationships.
- God has healed me (spirit, soul, and body).
- I can make it through every difficult circumstance by the power of Jesus Christ.
- I surround myself with positive, uplifting people.

Action Item(s):

1. Start a daily habit of beginning each day focusing on God. It could be five minutes of prayer or reading a chapter in the Bible. It's okay to start small and build up. Don't get hung up with the number of minutes. Just start somewhere and stick to it! Notice if your mood is better on the days you spend time with God first thing.

2. Begin your journey of surrounding yourself with positive people by joining a church group or meeting with an uplifting friend for lunch. If your friend can't make it, ask someone else. Don't give up. You can do it!

Are you enjoying this book?

Please take a quick minute to let other people know how great it is!

Scan the QR code to post your review now! Thanks so much!

CHAPTER 3

TOXIC ROMANCE UNVEILED

Have you ever been in a relationship that felt like you were constantly trying to decode a secret message, only to find out it was just a bunch of jumbled letters with no real meaning? Welcome to the world of toxic romance, where sometimes the love notes turn out to be warning signs. Let's not sugarcoat it; navigating these choppy waters can feel more like sailing into a storm. But you're not the captain of the Titanic, my friend. You've got this, and the first tool in your survival kit? Prayer.

In this chapter, we will look at some classic examples of toxic behaviors in romance: manipulation, isolation, love bombing, and gaslighting. I will reiterate that if you or your family members are in danger, please seek help and safety immediately. The topics in this chapter are serious; however, they do not address abusive relationships, whether physical, mental, emotional, verbal, or otherwise. Abuse, toxic marriage, and divorce are much deeper issues for future books.

However, if you are just beginning a romantic relationship and you spot signs of toxicity, you should walk away sooner rather than later. As we journey through this challenging chapter, I pray for your courage to recognize any possible warning signs of toxicity and take steps to mend or end the relationship. Let's do this!

Prayer: Our First Response

Imagine you've poured your heart into a relationship, but you start noticing red flags that tell you something isn't right. Your heart sinks because you've invested so much. But here's where a call to prayer and acceptance steps in. It's about seeking divine intervention, not just for the relationship's restoration, but also for the personal transformation of the one exhibiting toxic behaviors. Praying might feel like sending a distress signal into a vast, echoing space, wondering if it's heard. But here's the comforting part—God hears. And while He respects our free will, He also speaks to our hearts, often in ways we might not expect.

However, and this is a big however, change is a two-way street. It's crucial to realize that while you can hope, pray, and yearn for change in your partner, the decision to change rests with them. God gave us free will for a reason. If He controlled our every action, we'd be robots, programmed and predictable, not people capable of love and choice. This means that while you can (and should) pray for transformation, it's ultimately up to your partner to embrace that change.

This brings us to a much tougher action item: confrontation. Addressing toxic behavior is necessary. It's like gently, but firmly, pulling out those weeds. Be prepared because not everyone appreciates someone messing with their roots, even if those roots are a bit tangled. They might resent it, and yes, the relationship could even worsen. It's a risk but worth taking if it means a healthier space for both of you to grow. But always remember: you must be prepared for all outcomes, including the possibility of walking away from the relationship if necessary.

Navigating toxic romance is no walk in the park. It's more like a hike on a rocky path where every step must be taken carefully. But with prayer as your first response, you arm yourself with a powerful tool that illuminates the path, guides your steps, and keeps you anchored in hope and faith. So, lace up those hiking boots, my friend. Armed with prayer and God's Word, you're ready for the journey ahead, no matter how rugged the road.

Love Bombing vs. Genuine Affection: Distinguishing the Indistinguishable

Let's chat about something that often starts as sweet as a box of chocolates but can sometimes have a bitter aftertaste—love bombing. This is a form of relational manipulation where one person showers the other with overwhelming gifts and affection, often after a disagreement, to exert control. These times of extreme attention may be followed by periods of neglect or indifference for no apparent reason. Picture this: it's like someone showers you with a torrential downpour of affection, gifts, and sweet nothings, so much so that you might feel like you're starring in your own personal rom-com. But here's the twist—not all grand romantic gestures are created equal. At its core, love bombing isn't about genuine care but control. It's like someone giving you an umbrella not to shield you from the rain but to keep you under their control, dictating when to open it and when to fold it away.

On the flip side, there's genuine affection—this is the real deal. This kind of love is about mutual growth and respect. It feels like sunshine on your face—a warm, nourishing light that encourages you to bloom. It's consistent, without the roller-coaster highs followed by mysterious lows. Genuine affection involves a steady stream of care and consideration that respects your individuality rather than overwhelming it. It's the kind of affection that builds you up, cheers for your successes, and supports you through challenges without keeping a scorecard.

So, how do you tell the difference? It's all about the vibes and the consistency. Love bombing often feels like a whirlwind, whisking you off your feet before you know what's happening. It's intense and all-consuming, often coming into play when things need to be 'fixed' or smoothed over. For example, after a disagreement, a love bomber might suddenly shower you with gifts or affection to 'make up' for it, using grand gestures as a handy distraction from underlying issues.

Genuine affection, meanwhile, doesn't need to shout from the rooftops. It's the quiet, everyday actions that speak volumes—the morning texts just to say hello, the thoughtful gestures that show you're on their mind, and the consistent way they treat you with kindness, whether in public or in private. It's affection that's woven into the fabric of everyday life, not just used as glittery confetti thrown around to dazzle and distract.

God is very clear about what love should look like. 1 Corinthians 13:4-7 tells us that love is patient, and love is kind. It does not envy, it does not boast, it is not proud. It does not dishonor others; it is not self-seeking, is not easily angered, and keeps no record of wrongs. This passage doesn't describe love as an overwhelming flood that drowns out everything else. Instead, it paints a picture of love as a nurturing, respectful, and selfless partnership. If your relationship feels more like a tactical game of chess than a cooperative game of building something beautiful together, it might be time to reassess.

Understanding these dynamics is crucial for your emotional health and building lasting, loving relationships that reflect the kind of love God wants for us. It's about having the wisdom to discern the genuine from the counterfeit and the courage to embrace the kind of love that uplifts and sustains. Remember, real love doesn't overwhelm or undermine; it nurtures and supports. It's a gentle garden of growth, not a storm of flowers one day and thorns the next. So, as you navigate the waters of romance, keep your eyes open for the signs of genuine affection, and don't be afraid to exit if the rain of love bombs starts to pour. After all, the best relationships are built on the solid ground of mutual respect and genuine care, where every day feels a little bit like sunshine.

Confronting Gaslighting: Strategies for Reclaiming Your Reality

Now, let's tackle that sneaky beast we mentioned earlier that can make you question your sanity: gaslighting. Picture this: You're telling your loved one about something upsetting that happened, and instead of support, you get, "Oh, it wasn't that bad," or "You're just too sensitive." At first, it might not bug you much, but over time, these comments accumulate like unwelcome house guests, making you doubt your feelings and memories. Gaslighting is this psychological sleight of hand, a form of manipulation so subtle and persistent that it can shake the very foundation of your reality.

The term "gaslighting" comes from the 1944 movie *Gaslight*, in which a man convinces his wife to doubt her sanity. She asks him why the gas lights are dimming in their home, which, unbeknownst to her, he is causing in an attempt to commit some nefarious deed. By telling her she is crazy and what she is experiencing is not happening, he actually convinces her that she is going insane. It is a manipulation tactic that can, unfortunately, be very effective.

So, why is it essential to understand gaslighting? Because, my friend, knowing is half the battle. Recognizing that you're being gaslighted is like turning on a light in a dim room. Suddenly, you see what's been tripping you up all this time, and you can start navigating your space more safely. Gaslighting thrives in shadows and confusion, so clarity becomes your powerful ally. In these moments, remember the words of Ephesians 4:25, "Therefore each of you must put off falsehood and speak truthfully to your neighbor, for we are all members of one body." This Scripture isn't just about not lying; it's a call to embrace and speak truth to ourselves and others, which is the antithesis of gaslighting.

So, what can you do to reclaim your reality and detoxify your environment from gaslighting? First off, grab your notebook and pen again. Journaling is more than just venting; it's a validation of your experiences and feelings. Every time you jot down what happened and how it made you feel, you build a personal archive saying, "This is the truth." When someone tries to repaint your reality, you have your own unaltered version of events, written in your hand, that no one can erase or overwrite. Obviously, gaslighting can turn into emotional abuse, so you must use discernment in your own personal situation when it comes to confrontation, setting boundaries, and ending the relationship for your well being.

Seeking counsel is another wise strategy. This could be a pastor, a trusted friend, or a Christian counselor—someone who can provide perspective without being emotionally entangled in the situation. These conversations can be eye-opening, offering new angles to view your experiences and reminding you that you're not navigating this alone. Proverbs 11:14 says, "Where there is no guidance, a people falls, but in an abundance of counselors there is safety." This safety isn't just about comfort but stability and clarity—two things desperately needed when recovering from gaslighting.

Just be careful about the people with whom you share personal details. Make sure they are trustworthy and will not repeat what they hear. Also, watch your headspace when sharing. Make sure you're calm and controlled and have had time to assess the matter independently instead of blurting everything out when you're in the heat of anger. An emotional outburst could cause severe repercussions in the relationship. A general rule is to wait a few days after an argument to pray and process what happened before seeking godly counsel. It is amazing how your perspective can shift after your emotions calm down.

Please note: This waiting period does not apply if you are being abused in any way, in which case you should seek immediate help and safety.

Strengthening your relationship with Jesus is the most crucial component of all. This means weaving prayer and Scripture into your daily routine, which fortifies your spirit and sharpens your discernment. When you're grounded in your faith, it's like having a built-in truth detector. You become more attuned to discrepancies between what you know to be right and what a toxic individual is telling you. Faith isn't just about believing in what we cannot see; it's about trusting in the truths that have stood the test of time—even when someone tries to convince you otherwise.

Tackling gaslighting is a process, often a delicate dance of reclaiming your thoughts and healing your perspective. But with these tools—prayer, journaling, seeking counsel, and strengthening your relationship with Jesus—you are well-equipped to clear the fog and redirect the narrative of your life toward truth. Remember, every step you take towards understanding and addressing gaslighting is a step towards not just surviving but thriving in the truth of who you are and the world you live in. So keep these strategies close, like arrows in your quiver, ready to defend your reality and shoot down any attempts to distort it. With truth as your compass, you're more than capable of navigating even the trickiest relational landscapes.

Breaking Free: A Faith-based Approach to Leaving Toxic Romantic Relationships

Sometimes, the most challenging thing and the right thing are the same. Deciding to leave a romantic relationship that drains your spirit rather than fills it can feel like trying to climb out of a bottomless, muddy pit—you know you need to get out, but where do you even begin? It's a tough spot, no doubt about it. But recognizing when to say goodbye is the first crucial step to reclaiming your peace and well-being. Let's talk about those red flags that scream, "It's time to move on!"

Recognizing when to exit the relationship often comes down to a few soul-check questions: Does this relationship bring me closer to the person God has called me to be, or does it pull me into being someone I don't even recognize? Am I thriving, or am I merely surviving? If you dread interactions that should bring joy or constantly feel diminished, criticized, or emotionally manipulated, these are billboard-sized signs pointing toward the exit. It's like when you keep ignoring your car's check engine light; eventually, you're going to end up stranded on the side of the road. Don't wait for your emotional engine to break down before you decide to take action.

If you have determined it's time to walk away, rely on Christ to help you through this challenging departure. Remember, the same God who parted the Red Sea to lead His people out of Egypt can make a way for you out of a toxic relationship. It's about leaning into that faith, letting it embolden you to take steps that might seem impossible. Pray for courage, seek wisdom in Scripture, and trust that you're not walking this path alone. Psalms 46:1 reminds us, "God is our refuge and strength, an ever-present help in trouble." That's not just poetic; it's a promise you can stand on.

Navigating an exit from a toxic relationship is rarely easy. But with a clear recognition of when it's time to leave and a deep reliance on your relationship with Jesus, you can steer towards a future where peace and joy aren't just occasional visitors but permanent residents. So, take that first step, knowing that each move towards freeing yourself from toxicity is a move towards reclaiming the beautiful story God has written for your life.

. . .

Healing After Heartbreak: Rebuilding Self-Worth with God's Love

After the storm clouds of a toxic relationship have cleared, you might find yourself sorting through the emotional debris, wondering how to start rebuilding. It's like standing in the ruins of a once vibrant garden, where everything familiar seems irreversibly damaged. But here's the good news: the seeds of self-worth and renewal are still there, waiting to be nurtured back to life, and divine love is the sunshine that makes that possible.

Understanding God's unconditional love is like discovering a wellspring in the desert. It's vital for quenching that deep-seated thirst for acceptance and value that toxic relationships often leave behind. When you grasp how deeply and unconditionally God loves you, it's like putting on a pair of glasses that corrects distorted vision. Suddenly, you see yourself not as a collection of flaws or failures but as a beloved child of God, cherished and worthy of respect and kindness. This divine perspective is transformative—it rebuilds the foundation of your self-worth, reminding you that your value isn't based on someone else's opinion of you or even on your own sometimes harsh self-judgments but on something far more enduring.

Embracing practical actions can help cement this new understanding of your worth. Start with Scriptural affirmations—they're like medicine for the soul. Verses like Psalm 139:14, where you're reminded that you are "fearfully and wonderfully made," can become daily affirmations that reinforce a positive, loving view of yourself. Speak these truths over your life, write them on post-it notes, and stick them where you'll see them often—like your bathroom mirror or fridge door. Surround yourself with constant reminders of your inherent worth.

Community involvement is another healing balm. Engaging

with others who are walking paths of faith and love can significantly strengthen your sense of belonging and purpose. Whether it's joining a church group, volunteering, or simply spending more time with family and friends who uplift you, each positive interaction is a step towards reinforcing your self-worth and healing your heart.

Avoiding future toxicity is crucial as you move forward. Now that you're beginning to see your worth through the lens of divine love, you'll be better equipped to recognize relationships that don't honor this new understanding. It's like having a detector that beeps loudly when toxic behaviors are near. You will be okay with being alone rather than being in a toxic relationship because you have learned to like yourself. And you will realize that when you have a personal relationship with Jesus Christ, you are never truly alone. He is always with you. Remember, maintaining freedom from toxicity is not a one-time event but an ongoing process—regular self-reflection, ongoing community support, and a deepening relationship with Jesus Christ are all part of the maintenance work.

Let's not forget the power of testimonies in this healing journey. Hearing stories from others who have navigated similar paths can be incredibly encouraging. For instance, consider Shelly, who, after years in a demeaning relationship, found strength through prayer groups and Scripture to rediscover her joy and self-worth. Or John, who used his faith in Christ to overcome the scars left by emotional abuse and is now helping others in his church community through similar struggles. These stories aren't just tales of survival; they're beacons of hope, shining light on the path to healing and reminding you that recovery isn't just possible; it's promised.

The road to recovery from a toxic relationship might be long and winding, but it's lined with God's steadfast love and support. Each step you take towards healing, reinforced by divine love, is a step towards a brighter, more fulfilling future. You are not defined by your past relationships but by the unshakeable love of God. With this divine foundation, you can start to rebuild, knowing that your worth is rooted not in imperfection but in the perfect love that calls you its own.

As we close this chapter on healing after heartbreak, we carry forward the lessons of divine love, drawing near to Christ, and community support. These are not just steps toward recovery; they are strides toward a deeper, more meaningful life. So, as you turn the page, take these truths with you, let them infuse your future with hope, and prepare to step into the next chapter of your life, fortified, renewed, and deeply loved.

* * *

Reflection Questions:

Is my romantic relationship centered on Christ?

Does my romantic relationship build me up or tear me down?

If my romantic relationship is not a marriage, is it time to walk away?

If my marriage is toxic, what can I do to improve the relationship? Is it time to seek professional Biblical counsel?

* * *

Related Scriptures:

Be strong and courageous. Do not be afraid or terrified because of

them, for the Lord your God goes with you; He will never leave
you nor forsake you (Deuteronomy 31:6, NIV).

So don't be afraid; you are worth more than many sparrows
(Matthew 10:31, NIV).

You are altogether beautiful, my darling; there is no flaw in you
(Song of Songs 4:7, NIV).

I will praise Thee; for I am fearfully and wonderfully made:
Marvelous are Thy works; And that my soul knoweth right well
(Psalms 139:14, KJV).

If possible, as far as it depends on you, live at peace with everyone
(Romans 12:18, AMPC).

For the Lord, the God of Israel, says: I hate divorce *and* marital
separation and him who covers his garment [his wife] with
violence. Therefore keep a watch upon your spirit [that it may be
controlled by My Spirit], that you deal not treacherously *and*
faithlessly [with your marriage mate] (Malachi 2:16, AMPC).

Affirmations to Speak Aloud:
In the Name of Jesus, I declare:

- I am loved by God.
- He loves me so much that He gave His Son to die for me.
- I see myself the way God sees me: beautiful, worthy of
  love, fearfully and wonderfully made.
- I will wait as long as needed for the relationship God has
  ordained for me.

- I am okay with not being in a romantic relationship because I have Jesus, and He is more than enough for me.

* * *

Action Item(s):

After prayer and listening for direction from God, if you have determined that your romantic relationship is toxic, take a step towards freedom today. If you are not married, confront your romantic partner and walk away if necessary. If you are married, confront your spouse and seek professional Biblical counseling.

CHAPTER 4

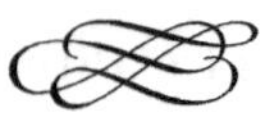

NAVIGATING TOXIC FAMILY DYNAMICS

Do you ever feel like family gatherings should come with a safety manual? "In case of unsolicited advice, break glass and sound an alarm!" Jokes aside, while family is often our backbone, providing love and support, it can sometimes feel like they're more like thorns in our flesh. This chapter is about untangling those knots—understanding, addressing, and healing from family toxicity. It's about recognizing that even the garden of family love can sometimes grow weeds, and it's up to us to tend to it.

Identifying Toxicity in Family Ties: A Closer Look

Navigating family dynamics is akin to walking through a minefield blindfolded—you know there are explosives around, but you can't see them until it's too late. From the moment we're born, our families play a pivotal role in shaping who we are, from teaching us how to tie our shoelaces to influencing our worldviews. But what happens when the people who are supposed to uplift us end up doing the opposite? Recognizing and accepting that a family relationship is causing more harm than good can feel like betraying family loyalty, but it's a crucial step towards healthier interactions.

First, let's tackle the unique challenges of spotting toxicity within family dynamics. It's tricky because, unlike friendships or romantic relationships where you can see things somewhat objectively, family relationships are steeped in history, emotions, and, let's be honest, a lot of baggage. There's also the unspoken rule about family loyalty, which can make calling out toxic behaviors feel like you're rocking the boat on calm seas. But remember, acknowledging the water is choppy is the first step to steering the ship to smoother waters.

Now, let's move on to the patterns of toxicity that are often specific to families. Maybe it's the overbearing parent who still treats you like you're twelve, dictating your choices from how you raise your kids to how you clean your house, or the sibling whose competitiveness leaves little room for genuine happiness about your successes. These behaviors can range from subtle comments that undercut your self-esteem to more overt actions like manipulation or emotional blackmail (think guilt trips served up at family dinners). Recognizing these patterns is like learning to read a complex weather map; once you know what to look for, you can better predict storms and navigate safely.

From a Biblical perspective, honoring our parents and loving our siblings are teachings woven into the fabric of Scripture. Yet, the Bible doesn't call us to endure toxic behaviors under the guise of honor. Ephesians 4:2-3 teaches us to "Be completely humble and gentle; be patient, bearing with one another in love. Make every effort to keep the unity of the Spirit through the bond of peace." This directive includes maintaining our own peace and mental health. It's about finding a balance between upholding Biblical principles and ensuring we're not spiritually or emotionally depleted.

So, how do we strike that balance? It begins with setting clear boundaries, which we'll explore more later. But it's also about open, honest communication and, sometimes, agreeing to disagree. It's about recognizing that loving someone doesn't always mean having them close—it can also mean loving them from a distance while you work on healing and preserving your well-being.

Interactive Element: Family Dynamics Journal Prompt

To help you reflect and navigate your family dynamics, here's a journal prompt to explore:

Reflect on a recent family interaction that felt unhealthy:

- Describe the scenario: What was said or done that made you feel uncomfortable or hurt?
- Analyze the impact: How did this interaction affect your emotional and mental state?
- Plan a response: What are some healthy ways you can address this if it happens again?

This exercise isn't just about venting (although that's perfectly fine); it's about shifting from reaction to response. By understanding how toxicity manifests in your family, you can better prepare and protect yourself. Remember, maintaining your mental and spiritual health isn't selfish—it's necessary and allows you to engage with your family in more meaningful and healthy ways.

In navigating these family waters, keep your compass on love, understanding, and forgiveness, but also on boundaries. It's a delicate dance, but with the proper steps, you can maintain balance and ensure that your family ties are supportive, not suffocating.

Honoring Your Parents While Protecting Your Peace

So you're trying to navigate the tricky waters of family dynamics, especially with your folks, and it feels like trying to bake a soufflé in a home economics class taught by Gordon Ramsay—intense, high-stakes, and a little nerve-wracking, huh? Well, let's put on our aprons and get to it. Honoring your parents is a commandment we know well, but it gets super complicated when their behavior might be the reason you're stress-eating cupcakes at midnight.

Honoring your parents doesn't mean you have to endure toxicity with a smile. It's about showing respect, yes, but also about maintaining your well-being. It's like trying to keep your garden flourishing—sometimes, you must prune back the old to let the new thrive. The Bible encourages us to honor our father and mother so that our days may be long (Ephesians 6:2-3), but it doesn't say we must lose ourselves in the process. Think of Jesus and His interactions; even He had moments where He had to lay down boundaries. Remember when He had to take time away from even His disciples to pray?

Setting boundaries with parents might sound like you're setting up a war zone, but it's more about building a peace treaty. For instance, if your mom has the habit of calling you multiple times a day and it's stressing you out, set clear, loving limits. You might say, "Mom, I love our chats, but I can only handle calls in the evening after work." The key? Keep your communication as clear as your grandma's crystal and as soft as her homemade quilts. It's not about being defensive; it's about being assertive—there's a big difference, and it lies in the tone and intention.

Navigating these conversations can be tricky. Start by choosing a good time—bringing up a sensitive topic right before Dad cuts into the Thanksgiving turkey? Not ideal. Approach the conversation with empathy and clarity. Acknowledge their feelings, but express your own needs. You might say, "I know you worry about me, and I appreciate your advice, but I need to make my own decisions about my career. I value your support as I navigate these choices." It's about affirming their role in your life while also standing firm in your autonomy.

Now, let's talk about self-care because, let's face it, dealing with family dynamics can be draining. It's like running a marathon; you need to keep hydrated. Only in this case, your hydration is self-care. This can look like setting aside time after a family gathering to decompress or saying no to events that leave you more frazzled than festive. By the way, it's okay to say no! You have permission not to attend every family gathering or event throughout the year. Maybe they'll be disappointed; perhaps they'll gossip about you. Oh well. They will do that anyway, whether you attend the event or not. So do what you want to do. Don't live your life trying to fulfill someone else's impossible expectations of you. It's about acknowledging that you're human and you have limits. Just as you wouldn't drive a car without changing its oil, don't push through family issues without giving yourself a tune-up.

Lastly, don't underestimate the power of seeking external support. Whether it's friends who get it, a counselor who listens, or a Bible study group where you can receive Biblical advice, having an external sounding board can provide invaluable perspectives and coping strategies. It's like having a cheer squad, but instead of pom-poms, they're armed with tissues, chocolate, and sound advice.

Navigating the commandment to honor your parents while protecting your peace is a delicate balancing act. It requires grace, patience, and consistency. But remember, you're not doing this alone. Every step you take towards healthier family dynamics is a step towards a healthier you, and that's something worth striving for. So, keep your head up and your boundaries firm. After all, peace isn't just something you find; it's something you create, one conversation at a time.

. . .

Sibling Rivalry: Cain and Abel in the Modern World

Ah, siblings. They can be our first friends and our first rivals. If you've ever had a spat over who gets the last slice of pizza or whose turn it is to use the bathroom first, you know that sibling relationships are a complex dance of love, competition, and everything in between. But when does this rivalry cross the line into something more toxic? Let's take a page from one of the oldest sibling stories known to us—Cain and Abel—and explore how ancient lessons can illuminate our modern family dramas.

Sibling rivalry isn't just about who mom and dad love best or who got the bigger birthday cake. At its core, it's about competition for resources, whether those resources are parental attention, affection, or approval. In the story of Cain and Abel, we see the dangers of letting this rivalry fester, leading Cain to commit the ultimate act of violence against his brother Abel. While most sibling rivalries don't lead to such extreme outcomes, the story highlights the potential for escalating conflict when feelings of jealousy and competition are left unchecked.

Understanding the roots of sibling rivalry involves peeling back the layers of these relationships to reveal the fears and desires driving them. Often, what looks like petty arguments over trivial things are expressions of deeper needs for validation and love. It's like when you're hangry (hungry + angry) and snap at someone; it's not really about the momentary annoyance; it's about a deeper need not being met. Similarly, when siblings fight, it might not just be about who gets control of the TV remote; it's about feeling seen and valued.

Healing these relationships starts with recognizing and addressing the underlying issues. Strategies for healing can include setting up family meetings to ensure everyone has a chance to voice their feelings in a safe space. Think of it as a 'peace summit' where everyone comes to the table not to negotiate a ceasefire but to understand each other's perspectives and needs. It's about moving from competition to cooperation, where the family unit works like a team, each member rooting for the other's success.

Preventing toxic sibling rivalry begins early in childhood. Parents can play a crucial role by fostering an environment where each child's unique talents and qualities are celebrated rather than pitting one child against another. This might involve conscious efforts to spend individual time with each child, affirming their value outside their achievements or behaviors. It's about laying the groundwork for a family culture that values collaboration over competition, where siblings see each other as allies rather than adversaries. Remember, it's never too late to rebuild sibling relationships. I've seen adults in their 70s move beyond past hurts and create amazing friendships with their siblings. Never give up on having a very special relationship with your siblings. God can heal all hurts!

Interactive Element: Forgiveness Exercise

To foster forgiveness and strengthen sibling bonds, try this simple exercise:

1. Reflect: Think about a recent conflict with your sibling. What emotions did you feel? What needs were not being met?
2. Dig deeper: Was the conflict the real cause of your frustration towards your sibling, or was it something else? Something deeper, something from the past? Be honest. Ask God to show you the root of the issue if it is unclear. Is your sibling just annoying? Are they your parents' favorite? Were they always prettier or more successful than you? Did they hurt you? Did they

disapprove of you? Whatever it is, find the root of your feelings towards your sibling. If you are in the wrong, repent and move on. If they are in the wrong, forgive and move on. If it's both, do both. It's not worth living in bitterness, resentment, and pain. Choose freedom for yourself!

3. Write: Write a letter to your sibling expressing your feelings about the conflict, but do not send it. This is just for you to articulate your emotions.

4. Meet: Arrange a time to talk with your sibling. Start the conversation with affirmations and things you appreciate about them.

5. Discuss: Share your feelings calmly and listen to their side of the story. Aim for understanding, not winning.

6. Plan: Together, brainstorm some ways to avoid similar conflicts in the future. Maybe it's a code word when things get heated or a promise to give each other time to cool down before discussing issues.

Forgiveness is not about erasing the past but building a bridge to a better future. It involves acknowledging the hurt and choosing to mend the relationship despite it. As siblings work through these steps, they lay down the stepping stones of forgiveness and understanding, paving the way for stronger, more loving relationships.

In navigating the complex waters of sibling relationships, remember that every family is unique, and there's no one-size-fits-all solution. But with a commitment to understanding, forgiveness, and proactive communication, siblings can transform rivalry into a lifelong friendship. After all, who better to share your journey with than those who have been by your side from the beginning? So, here's to siblings—the ones who know us best, challenge us hardest, and love us most fiercely. Make an effort to mend the relationship. Be the bigger person. Give more than you receive. When you stand before God one day, you won't regret any action you took in the name of peace and love.

Setting Boundaries with Family: A Step-by-Step Perspective

Have you ever tried to explain to your family why you need a little personal space without causing a mini-drama series? It's like trying to sneak out of a family reunion early; someone will notice, and there might be some hurt feelings. But here's the thing: setting boundaries is not just about carving out "me time." It's about cultivating personal and spiritual growth. Just as a gardener fences off a new plant to protect it from trampling feet, setting boundaries protects your emotional space from being trampled upon. It's essential, and yes, it's also Biblical.

Remember when Jesus went off to pray alone, leaving His disciples behind? Even He needed space to connect with God and replenish His spirit (Mark 1:35). What about when Mary chose to sit at Jesus's feet while Martha was busy in the kitchen? Jesus affirmed Mary's choice to set a boundary around her time and focus on what was better (Luke 10:42). These moments in Scripture highlight the importance of setting boundaries for practical reasons and spiritual nourishment and growth.

So, how do you set these boundaries without setting off alarms? First, identify what you need from your family interactions and what you don't. Maybe you decide that Grandma's visits are lovely, but daily drop-ins are too much. Or perhaps you find that discussions about your weight or marital status with relatives are off-limits because they leave you feeling judged rather than loved. Recognizing these needs is like mapping out a garden; you must know what you're planting to understand where to put the fences.

Next, have the boundary talk. It's about being as transparent with your family as a cloudless sky. Start by affirming your love and respect for them because starting on a positive note can help prevent the conversation from becoming a defensive battle. Explain your needs calmly and clearly, like, "I love our chats, Mom, but I'm most refreshed and present during our conversations when we keep them to around thirty minutes." Be prepared to also listen to their feelings and responses. This isn't a monologue; it's a dialogue.

Handling pushback is where things can get prickly. Expect some resistance when you first set boundaries, especially if it's new to your family dynamics. You might feel guilty, like you're doing something wrong by asking for some space. Remember, guilt is a common initial reaction, especially if you're used to putting others' needs before your own. But it's crucial to stand firm, knowing that setting boundaries is not just for your well-being but also for the health of your relationships. It's better to face a bit of guilt now than to harbor resentment later, which can do long-term damage to your relationships.

Navigating this resistance is like being a weather forecaster; you must anticipate and prepare. Keep your explanations simple and your emotions in check. Reinforce why these boundaries are necessary for your happiness and spiritual growth. You could say, "When I have time to myself in the evenings to read or pray, I feel more centered and more present with you all during our time together." Over time, as they see the positive outcomes of your boundaries, their resistance may turn into respect.

Setting boundaries with family isn't about building walls but drawing lines in the sand where the tide can't erase them. It's about loving yourself and your family enough to say, "This far and no further." As you do, you're protecting your peace and cultivating an environment where love, respect, and personal growth can flourish. So, gently but firmly hold your boundary lines, and watch your relationships grow healthier like a well-tended garden.

. . .

Confronting Familial Toxicity: Balancing Love and Self-Preservation

Imagine you're at a family gathering where the air is thick with the aroma of grandma's famous casserole and the subtle tension that always seems to simmer beneath the surface. Perhaps it's that one uncle whose jokes are more hurtful than humorous or a cousin who never misses a chance to highlight your past mistakes. Confronting these moments isn't just about clearing the air; it's about maintaining your emotional and spiritual health. It's a delicate dance. But with a dash of compassion and a spoonful of assertiveness, you can serve some much-needed change at the next family feast.

When it comes to confronting toxic family members, think of it as choosing to heal a wound rather than letting it fester. The key ingredient here is compassion. This doesn't mean excusing their behavior but instead approaching the situation with an understanding that their toxicity often stems from their own unresolved issues or pain. It's like understanding why the stove is hot; you don't touch it out of spite but need to handle it with care. When you address the issue, ensure your words are seasoned with as much kindness as firmness. You might say, "I know you might not realize this, but your commenting on my career choices makes me feel belittled. I value your interest in my life, but I'd appreciate it if we could discuss it in a more supportive way."

In these confrontations, Scriptural backing can be incredibly reassuring. Consider Galatians 6:1, which instructs us to "restore someone gently." This gentle restoration isn't just about correcting them but doing so in a way that upholds their dignity and your own. It's a reminder that tough love isn't about toughness alone; the love part is just as crucial. It's about aiming for healing over winning an argument. It's challenging, especially when emotions run high and old patterns die hard. But remember, every word spoken with gentleness can be like a bridge over troubled waters, offering a path back to mutual respect and understanding.

Preparing for these confrontations is like gearing up for a major performance. Your heart's racing, you've got butterflies in your stomach, and everything feels a bit too real. This is where your emotional and spiritual prep comes into play. Spend time in prayer and ask God for peace and clarity. Dive into Scriptures that fortify your spirit and prepare your heart, such as Ephesians 4:15, which encourages speaking the truth in love. Keep your motives focused on healing and understanding rather than simply airing grievances. This spiritual armor will protect you and guide you in delivering your message in a way that's likely to be heard and received.

Forgiveness is the final course in this feast of familial confrontation and possibly the most complex dish to digest. Forgiving isn't about glossing over what happened or pretending everything is fine. It's about freeing your heart from the burden of bitterness. This doesn't necessarily mean reconciliation, especially if the toxic behaviors continue. Sometimes, forgiveness means taking a step back and loving from a distance. It's a personal journey involving a lot of letting go and letting God. Each act of forgiveness is a step towards healing, not just for you but potentially for your family members, too. It's about breaking the cycle, not just enduring it.

Navigating familial toxicity with a blend of love and self-preservation isn't easy. It requires a fierce and tender heart, strong enough to confront but soft enough to forgive. It's a balancing act of epic proportions but one well worth mastering. As you move forward, remember that each conversation, boundary set, and moment of forgiveness is a step towards surviving family dynamics and thriving within them. So, take a deep breath, arm yourself with compassion, and step into those conversations with a spirit geared toward healing and hope. Here's to turning family gatherings from battlegrounds into bonding places, one heartfelt conversation at a time!

Healing Your Inner Child: Reclaiming Peace Through Faith

When it comes to family, isn't it wild how decades-old dynamics can still make us feel like we're back in footie pajamas, struggling to reach the cookie jar? Those sweet and sour childhood moments shape much of who we are today. But what happens when those sour bits start overshadowing the sweet ones? Addressing and healing the wounds inflicted by family dynamics isn't about digging up old dirt; it's about cleaning out the wounds so they can finally heal properly, and yes, it's about letting that inner child of yours come out to play again, unafraid and unscarred.

Imagine this: your childhood experiences are like a series of old VHS tapes playing old movies in your mind. Some of these films are full of laughter and sunshine, while others might be tinged with sadness or fear. These tapes, especially the not-so-great ones, can have a sneaky way of influencing how you view the world and yourself, even years after they were first recorded. Addressing these past hurts starts with pressing the pause button and acknowledging they exist. It's like finally turning down the volume on that noisy old movie playing in the background of your life, distracting you from the beautiful new scenes you could be filming.

Let your faith in Jesus be the director in this healing process. It invites a narrative of forgiveness and redemption, reminding you that your past chapters don't have to define the rest of your story. This could look like meditating on Scriptures that affirm your worth and God's love for you, such as Psalm 139:14, which marvels at how wonderfully you are made. It's about replacing the critical voices of the past with the soothing, affirming voice of God's Word.

Therapeutic practices can be fantastic co-stars in this healing journey. Counseling, for instance, can provide a safe space to unpack those old films under the guidance of a professional who can help you sort through the scenes, identify the ones that caused the hurt, and rewrite the scripts. Support groups offer another layer of healing, connecting you with others who know firsthand what it's like to live with similar scripts. Together, you can share experiences, coping strategies, and victories. It's like having a team of scriptwriters and producers working with you to create a new, healthier narrative.

Finally, restoration and renewal are about taking all these healing steps and turning them into a daily practice that continuously nourishes your inner child. It's about creating new experiences and memories that can overwrite the old, painful ones. Each positive experience is like a patch of sunlight breaking through the clouds, slowly but surely brightening the once-shadowy landscapes of your childhood memories. Whether it's through creating new family traditions, setting aside time for activities that bring you joy, or simply allowing yourself moments of childlike wonder and play, these practices reinforce the healing and growth you've been nurturing.

Healing the inner child is a tender process. It requires patience and persistence. But as you engage in this healing work, supported by your faith in God and His Word, you'll find that the peace you reclaim isn't just for your inner child—it's for you, here and now, in every step you take and every new scene you create in the beautiful ongoing movie of your life. So, let the healing be thorough and the renewal joyful. Your inner child deserves no less, and neither do you.

. . .

Breaking Generational Curses: A Path to Freedom

Do you ever feel like you're living out a script written generations before you were born? Like there's an invisible force dictating the patterns of your family's drama, and somehow, you're expected to play along? Well, you're not just imagining things. Sometimes, families carry burdens from one generation to the next, creating what are known as generational curses. These aren't curses in the witchy sense but rather toxic patterns and behaviors that have become so ingrained in the family fabric that they seem almost normal. But here's the good news—you have power through Christ to break these cycles and chart a new course for yourself and future generations.

First up is recognizing these patterns. It starts with a bit of family research. Look back at your family history. Are there recurring themes of conflict, addiction, or even specific health issues? Maybe it's how anger is handled or perhaps a tendency towards isolation when things get tough. These aren't just quirks or coincidences; they're clues. Understanding these can sometimes feel like trying to solve a puzzle with half the pieces missing. Still, every bit you piece together provides more insight into the behaviors that have shadowed your family tree.

Now, onto the battle plan—spiritual warfare. This might sound like something out of a medieval playbook, but it's about using God's Word to confront and overcome these deep-seated issues. It involves prayer and spiritual assertiveness. It's standing your ground and saying, "This ends with me." Engaging in this type of prayer isn't just about asking for things to change; it's about recognizing the power God has given you through Jesus to enact that change.

Envision yourself as a warrior, armed not with physical weapons but with the sword of the Spirit, which is the Word of God, ready to defend your future and your loved ones from the cycles that have confined your family for too long. "It is for freedom that Christ has set us free. Stand firm, then, and do not let yourselves be burdened again by a yoke of slavery" (Galatians 5:1). You have been set free from every generational curse or cycle of destructive habits by the shed blood of Jesus Christ. Claim your freedom, walk in it, and refuse to let the enemy's lies discourage you. Find Scriptures that speak to your family situation and stand on them. Do not give up. If the Word of God has promised it, believe it, and you will eventually see it come to pass. After doing all this, continue to stand (see Ephesians 6).

Now that you've discovered your freedom in Christ, it's time to create a new legacy. This is like writing a new script for a play that gets better with every generation. It involves intentional living—making conscious choices that align with the values you want to define your family going forward. This could look like setting new traditions celebrating openness and support or establishing new communication and conflict-resolution approaches. Every positive action you take sows seeds for a healthier family tree that will bear fruit long after you're gone.

Support and accountability from your Christian community are invaluable in this journey. Think of your church or small groups as your pit crew in a race. They're there to offer support, keep you stocked up on spiritual nourishment, and cheer you on. They can provide practical advice, emotional support, and direct intervention if things get tough. Plus, being accountable to someone helps you stay on track. It's easier to slip back into old habits when you're going it alone, but having someone to answer to can give you that extra push you need to keep moving forward.

Breaking generational curses isn't just about saying no to the past; it's about saying yes to a future filled with hope, healing, and transformation. It's a courageous journey that requires strength, perseverance, and an unshakeable faith in the Word of God. But remember, every step you take is a step towards freedom—not just for you, but for every generation that follows. So keep pressing forward, armed with love and faith, and watch as the chains of the past dissolve, replaced by a legacy of freedom and flourishing.

Building a Godly Legacy: Starting with Yourself

When you think about legacies, what springs to mind? Consider grand, sweeping tales of ancestors who traveled across continents or built businesses from scratch through hard work, ingenuity, and perseverance. Your legacy doesn't start with grandiose acts; it begins with you, right in the heart of your family. It's about the spiritual and emotional seeds you plant today, which will bloom in the lives of your family members tomorrow. So, how do you begin this process? It starts with personal transformation and moves through setting an example, investing in your family's spiritual and emotional health, and covering everything in prayer.

Imagine you're a gardener, but instead of flowers, you're growing virtues like kindness, patience, and love within yourself. This personal transformation is crucial because, let's face it, you can't pour from an empty cup. By nurturing these qualities in yourself, you're better equipped to contribute positively to your family dynamics. It's about embodying the fruits of the Spirit (Galatians 5:22-23) so profoundly that they start to spill over into your interactions with your family. Think of it as internal decor; the more beautiful and peaceful your inner world, the more it beautifies your external world.

Setting a godly example may sound daunting, like you must always be perfect. But here's a little secret: it's not about perfection; it's about direction. Are you consistently moving toward love, grace, and understanding? Even in the face of family toxicity, showing forgiveness instead of bitterness and patience instead of irritation can make all the difference. It's like being a thermostat rather than a thermometer; you set the temperature of the interactions, not just react to them. Your family will notice this. More importantly, they might even be inspired by it.

Investing in your family's spiritual and emotional health is like investing in a treasure that will yield future returns for generations. This could look like initiating family devotions, where you come together to read the Word, pray, or discuss current issues through a Biblical lens. Or it could be ensuring that open, honest communication is a staple at your dinner table. Every Scripture shared and every prayer offered is a brick in the foundation of a spiritually healthy home. It's about creating an environment where questions are encouraged, struggles can be shared, and support is readily given.

Speaking of prayer, never underestimate its power. Praying for your family is like placing a shield of divine protection around them. It's calling upon God's power to intervene in the complexities of your family life, to bless, protect, and guide each member. Whether it's praying for wisdom in dealing with a rebellious teen, reconciliation in a strained marriage, or peace amid family chaos, these prayers are potent. They weave a spiritual safety net, undergirding all your efforts to foster a godly legacy.

Building a godly legacy takes time, effort, and a lot of heart. But every step you take, from personal growth to setting a godly example, from investing in your family's hearts to covering them in prayer, brings you closer to having the family relationships you desire. Start with the person in the mirror and watch the ripples extend outward, touching everyone around you. Keep working on your relationships and watch God do amazing things.

As this chapter wraps, remember that the legacy you're building will stretch beyond the confines of your immediate family. It will seep into every interaction, every relationship, and yes, even into generations you might never meet. You're not just passing down genes; you're passing down a heritage of faith, hope, and love. So don't give up!

* * *

Reflection Questions:

Are any of my family members toxic? If so, who?

What can I do to strengthen toxic family relationships? (Examples: pray, forgive, let it go, set boundaries, confront them, seek Biblical counsel, etc.)

Are there any generational curses on my family? If so, list them and commit to praying for victory and freedom from these curses through the blood of Jesus.

* * *

Related Scriptures:

Finally, be strong in the Lord and in his mighty power. Put on the full armor of God, so that you can take your stand against the devil's schemes. For our struggle is not against flesh and blood, but against the rulers, against the authorities, against the powers of this dark world and against the spiritual forces of evil in the heavenly realms. Therefore put on the full armor of God, so that when the day of evil comes, you may be able to stand your ground, and after you have done everything, to stand. Stand firm then, with the belt of truth buckled around your waist, with the breastplate of righteousness in place, and with your feet fitted with the readiness that comes from the gospel of peace. In addition to all this, take up the shield of faith, with which you can extinguish all the flaming arrows of the evil one. Take the helmet of salvation and the sword of the Spirit, which is the word of God. And pray in the Spirit on all occasions with all kinds of prayers and requests.

With this in mind, be alert and always keep on praying for all the Lord's people (Ephesians 6:10-18, NIV).

***

Affirmations to Speak Aloud:

In the Name of Jesus, I declare:

- I love my family members.
- I have great relationships with all of them.
- I forgive them freely, for I have been forgiven.
- I am not easily offended or annoyed.
- I am easygoing and don't sweat the small stuff.
- My family has been set free from every generational curse through the power of Christ Jesus.

***

Actions Item(s):

Create a 'Family Blessing Box'. Each family member can write down prayers or blessings they wish for others on small pieces of paper and place them in the box. Choose a regular time each week to read them aloud together. This fosters a spirit of unity and support and reminds everyone of the power of prayer and positive intentions in your family's life.

CHAPTER 5

OVERCOMING TOXIC FRIENDSHIPS

Have you ever had a friend who, instead of being your cheerleader, seemed more like they were secretly rooting for your downfall? It's like having a personal trainer who eats donuts in front of you during a workout—confusing and just downright disrespectful! This chapter is all about those tricky waters of friendship that, instead of lifting us up, feel like they're pulling us under. So buckle up because we're diving into the complex world of friendships, where sometimes the line between "BFF" and "frenemy" can get a little too blurry for comfort.

Recognizing Toxic Friendships

Picture this: you're super excited to share some fantastic news—maybe your child just made the Honor Roll, or you're planning a fun family vacation. But when you tell your friend, their reaction is, "Oh, that's nice," in a tone that's as flat as a pancake. They express no excitement, no squeals, just a bland, disinterested reaction. This is just one tiny red flag that your friend might be veering into toxic territory. Recognizing a toxic friendship often starts with noticing that your interactions leave you more drained than energized. Instead of feeling supported, you feel criticized; instead of feeling understood, you feel judged. Whenever you hang out, you're bracing yourself for a subtle put-down or that passive-aggressive comment that will sting for days.

Now let's talk about the double whammy—how these toxic friendships can impact your self-esteem and faith journey. It's hard enough dealing with a friend who's about as supportive as a soggy paper bag, but when their negativity starts to make you doubt your worth or shake your faith, it's a signal you can't ignore. These friends might question why you spend so much time on your church activities or make fun of you for making faith-based choices. It's like every seed of doubt they plant is designed to sprout into a weed, threatening to choke your spiritual growth.

So, what does the Bible say about dealing with friends who lead you away from your faith and personal growth? Proverbs 13:20 warns us, "Walk with the wise and become wise, for a companion of fools suffers harm." This doesn't mean you should only have friends who share your exact beliefs and views, but it does emphasize the importance of surrounding yourself with people who uplift you and encourage your relationship with Christ. It's about choosing friends who respect your faith journey, even if theirs looks different, rather than those who would lead you into the weeds.

But here's the million-dollar question: Can you preserve a friendship once it shows signs of toxicity? The answer is more than a simple yes or no. It depends on whether the friend is open to dialogue. Are they willing to sit down and have a heart-to-heart about how their actions affect you? Change isn't just about one conversation; it's about seeing consistent effort over time. It's about that friend apologizing and adjusting their behavior. If you see genuine change, it's encouraging for the future of the friendship. But if the toxic patterns continue despite your best efforts, it might be time to love them from a distance. It's not giving up on them; it's refusing to let anyone steer you off the path God has laid out for your life.

Navigating the shifting sands of friendship—especially when they get a little muddy—is tricky. It requires a keen eye for red flags and a heart that is ready to forgive but also wise enough to recognize when patterns are too entrenched to change without hurting you further. In this dance of friendships, knowing the steps—when to step in, when to step back—can make all the difference between a waltz and a weary stumble. So, keep your dance shoes ready, your eyes open, and your heart guarded with the wisdom that comes from above. Here's to friendships that feel like two people rowing in the same direction, not one rowing and the other drilling holes in the boat!

Confronting a Toxic Friend: Conversations That Heal

Imagine you're gearing up to have a heart-to-heart with a friend whose antics have been more draining than a marathon viewing of sad movies. It's like preparing to tell someone their cooking could use less salt—delicate, necessary, and a bit nerve-wracking. Approaching this kind of conversation requires tact, a clear head, a game plan, and most importantly, time spent in prayer beforehand. Ask God to help you confront your friend in a loving but clear way, and ask Him to soften your friend's heart to receive what you have to say without becoming defensive. Remember that God gave us free will, so it is ultimately up to your friend to accept or reject what you say.

So, how do you start such a chat without turning it into the Third World War? It's all about setting the right tone and environment. Maybe it's at your favorite coffee shop, where the aroma of freshly brewed coffee might soften the forthcoming hard truths, or a quiet park bench where the open space could inspire openness in your dialogue.

When you initiate this conversation, it's crucial to come from a place of love and concern, not accusation. Start with affirmatives and observations rather than judgments. For instance, you might say, "I've noticed you've been really critical of me lately, and it's been pretty tough on me," rather than, "You're so negative all the time." This approach opens up space for dialogue instead of defensiveness. It's like offering someone a hand rather than a pointing finger. Scripturally, this mirrors Ephesians 4:15, where we're encouraged to speak the truth in love. This blend of honesty and gentleness can help maintain the friendship's integrity while addressing the issues head-on.

Setting realistic expectations for this conversation is like putting on your rain boots; it prepares you to handle the mud without getting your feet dirty. Understand that the outcome might not be an immediate resolution, and that's okay. Sometimes, these conversations are just starting points. Your friend might need time to process what you've said, just like sometimes, you need a moment to let a complex movie plot sink in. The goal here isn't necessarily to solve everything in one go but to start a constructive dialogue that could lead to more understanding and adjustment in behavior over time.

After you've navigated this tricky talk, remember to permit yourself to cool down. This might involve quiet time, praying and meditating on God's Word, or engaging in an activity that replenishes your spirit. Reflect on the conversation and consider jotting down any insights or feelings that emerged in a journal. This can be incredibly calming, helping you process and release any emotions stirred up by the exchange. Just like you might stretch after a physical workout to prevent stiffness, this post-conversation reflection can help prevent emotional 'stiffness' or lingering resentment. Congratulations on taking a big step toward mending the friendship!

In these moments of self-reflection, turn to your faith in Christ for strength and guidance. Philippians 4:6-7 reminds us not to be anxious about anything, but in every situation, by prayer and petition, with thanksgiving, present our requests to God. Let this assurance calm your spirit and gracefully reaffirm your resolve to handle the situation. Whether the outcome is positive or indicates that space is needed, lean on Jesus to provide the wisdom and peace you need to move forward.

Navigating the choppy waters of confronting a toxic friend isn't about burning bridges but reinforcing the foundations of respect and care in your friendships. It's about ensuring your social connections bring you closer to Christ, not tear you away. So take these steps with confidence, armed with empathy, prepared for any outcome, and secure in the knowledge that whatever the result, you're committed to healthier, uplifting interactions.

Letting Go and Growing: The Path to Healthier Friendships

Sometimes, holding on to a friendship that is dragging you down is like keeping an old concert ticket in your wallet—it's a memento of a fun time, but it won't get you into any new concerts. Understanding when to let a relationship go can be challenging, especially when you've shared so many memories. But just as seasons change, so do our dreams and goals, and recognizing the signs that a friendship is distracting you from those dreams and goals is crucial for your achieving the life God has designed for you to live.

Think of your friendships as plants in your garden. Some plants thrive and bloom year after year, while others might start to wither, no matter how much you water them. A friendship may fade when interactions consistently leave you feeling undervalued, hurt, or drained. It might be when you realize that your values have diverged to a point where every conversation feels like a subtle battle for moral high ground. Or it could be when you notice that your friend's presence in your life is stunting your spiritual growth rather than enriching it. When a friendship feels more like a chore or a series of painful compromises, it might be time to consider gently letting go, not with bitterness, but with a hope for new growth.

Letting go isn't just about endings; it's about creating space for new beginnings. Losing a toxic friendship can be surprisingly liberating, freeing up emotional and spiritual energy previously tangled up in managing the drama. This newfound energy can be spent on personal growth and exploring new interests that align more closely with what God has called you to accomplish. It's like pruning back the old branches in your garden to make room for new growth. You might discover forsaken talents or passions you had sidelined or find you're now more open to relationships that offer mutual support and encouragement. This period of growth can be a profoundly transformative time, where you learn more about the heart of God and what he has called you to do in life.

During this transition, finding support can make all the difference. Surrounding yourself with a community that understands and shares your faith can provide comfort and guidance. Whether it's your family, a church group, or Bible study partners, these networks offer a supportive environment where you can discuss your feelings and receive empathetic advice. They can also be a source of accountability, helping you to stay focused on your God-given dreams and goals. Engaging with a community that uplifts you can reinforce your decision to let go of toxic relationships, affirming that you deserve to be treated with kindness and respect.

Building new friendships might seem daunting, especially after a painful experience, but it's also an exciting opportunity to form connections more aligned with who you are now. When seeking new friends, look for qualities that reflect a healthy, godly relationship—honesty, kindness, generosity, and a shared commitment to growth. Start small by joining new groups or activities that interest you, and take the time to get to know people without rushing into deep friendships. Over time, these new friendships can develop into strong, supportive relationships that bring joy and encouragement.

Navigating the end of a toxic friendship and embracing the growth that comes from this change is a significant step in your spiritual and emotional journey. It's about making choices, prioritizing God's plan for your life, and trusting Him with your relationships. As you let go of the old and welcome the new, remember that each friendship, past and present, has a role in shaping who you are and aspire to be. So, take heart, keep nurturing your friendships, and watch them flourish into vibrant, uplifting places of refuge and encouragement.

Godly Friendships: What to Look For

So, what exactly makes up a godly friendship, and how can you cultivate such an enriching connection? First, godly friendships are marked by a commitment to each other's spiritual well-being. This doesn't mean you spend every coffee catch-up diving deep into theological debates—though those can be enriching, too! It's about encouraging each other to live out your faith in everyday actions. It's the friend who reminds you of God's love when you're feeling down or who prays for you when you're facing a challenge. These friends act like mirrors, reflecting God's love for you and helping you see His work in your life. They're the ones who stick by you, not just in times of joy, but also walk with you through valleys, always pointing you back to the light.

Now, how do you find these treasures when it seems so daunting? Faith communities are great places to look for such friendships. Churches, Bible study groups, and Christian events are not just social gatherings; they're places where people with a shared love for God come together. Get involved in activities that resonate with your interests and allow you to contribute your talents. Whether it's joining the choir, volunteering for church events, or attending Bible study sessions, each environment offers opportunities to connect with potential friends on a deeper level.

But friendships, like gardens, need maintenance to thrive. Keeping your godly friendships healthy involves a continuous give-and-take. It's about showing up for one another, not out of obligation, but out of genuine care and commitment. Respect each other's boundaries and be willing to offer support without overstepping. When conflicts arise—as they inevitably do in any relationship—address them honestly and gracefully. Remember, constructive communication is key. Approach misunderstandings with a heart ready to understand, not just to be understood. And always keep the lines of communication open, ensuring that you are both heard and listening.

Mutual accountability plays a critical role in maintaining the health of these friendships. It's about gently holding each other accountable to the values you profess, not in a judgmental way, but in a manner that encourages growth and improvement. This could look like checking in on each other's spiritual disciplines, offering gentle reminders to stay true to your faith in challenging times, or encouraging each other to act justly and love mercy, as Micah 6:8 advises. These friendships endure and empower you to become the best version of yourself, deeply rooted in faith and love.

As we wrap up this chapter on saying goodbye to toxic friendships and fostering godly friendships, remember that these relationships are a gift—not just companions for the road but co-travelers on a spiritual journey. They enrich your life, challenge you to grow, and reflect the love of Christ in both words and deeds. Cherish these friendships, invest in them, and watch as they transform your life and those around you.

With these seeds of wisdom, may you step into the next chapter of your life with a bouquet of flourishing friendships, each one strengthening your faith and brightening your path. Here's to vibrant friendships with joy and life, a testament to the beauty of shared trust and love.

Reflection Questions:

Who are my closest friends? Do these friends build me up or tear me down?

Should I confront or say goodbye to any toxic friends?

What can I do to strengthen my positive, uplifting friendships?

Related Scriptures:

A friend loves at all times, and is born, as is a brother, for adversity (Proverbs 17:17, AMPC).

Greater love has no one than this: to lay down one's life for one's friends (John 15:13, NIV).

One who has unreliable friends soon comes to ruin, but there is a friend who sticks closer than a brother (Proverbs 18:24, NIV).

Affirmations to Speak Aloud:

In the Name of Jesus, I declare:

- I am a joy to be around.
- Other people are drawn to me because of the light of Christ that radiates from me.
- I attract godly friends and companions.
- I am a good friend.
- I let go of any friendship that is distracting me from God's plan for my life.
- I forgive freely and wish the best for everyone.

Action Item(s):

To foster reflection and application, consider this simple exercise: Write down the names of three friends. Next to each name, jot down how they have helped you grow spiritually or how you might help each other to grow in faith. This exercise enables you to appreciate the value of each friendship and guides you in intentionally nurturing these relationships.

CHAPTER 6

TOXICITY IN THE WORKPLACE

Do you ever go to work in the mornings and feel like you're entering a wild jungle? There are predators (hello, office gossip mongers!), unexpected traps (sudden deadlines!), and you need to be as cunning as a fox to navigate the underbrush of office politics. Wouldn't it be nice to have a guidebook for dealing with workplace woes? Consider this chapter your modern-day, faith-fueled guide to handling workplace toxicity with grace and resilience.

Thriving in Difficult Work Environments

Remember Joseph from the Book of Genesis? He was sold into slavery by his jealous brothers, ended up in Egypt, and, through a series of divinely orchestrated events, rose to become the Pharaoh's right-hand man. Talk about a toxic workplace! Yet, Joseph thrived because he kept his integrity and leaned heavily on his faith. When you find yourself in tough spots at work, think of Joseph. He didn't let betrayal turn him bitter. Instead, he stayed true to his values and excelled at his tasks, even when the environment was less than ideal. His story is a powerful reminder that your response to adversity can be your most vital asset. You might not have control over the toxicity in your workplace, but like Joseph, you have control over your actions and attitudes. Let your work ethic, integrity, and faith speak for you. It might just change the course of your career, turning challenges into stepping stones.

Maintaining your integrity in a cutthroat environment is like trying to keep your white shirt clean while eating spaghetti—tricky, but not impossible. Start by setting clear personal boundaries about what you will and won't tolerate. Communicate these boundaries respectfully but firmly. For instance, if you're pressured to cut corners or engage in unfair practices, be like Joseph and stand your ground, even if it's unpopular. You can also seek allies who share your values, as there's strength in numbers. Together, you can support each other in maintaining a standard of integrity that might inspire change in your workplace culture.

Jealousy in the workplace can be as toxic as a bad apple in a fruit basket—it doesn't take much for the rot to spread. Remember Joseph's humility and resilience if you are targeted because of your success or ethics. He didn't brag about his achievements or special relationship with God, which might have fueled further jealousy. Instead, keep your accomplishments low-key, share credit generously, and focus on including others. When dealing with betrayal, take the high road. If possible, address the issue directly with those involved and seek resolution. If that fails, let your work speak for itself. Sometimes, like Joseph, you'll find that staying consistent in your integrity and dedication can bring about its rewards, often leading those who were once against you to respect and support you.

Joseph's ascent from a prisoner to a prime minister wasn't just luck but divine favor. In your career, invite God into every aspect of your work life. Start your day by spending time in God's Word and prayer, asking God to guide your decisions, bless your projects, and help you handle conflicts with grace. Reflect on Scriptures that promise God's favor, such as Psalm 5:12, which assures that the Lord blesses the righteous and surrounds them with favor. Remember, seeking God's favor doesn't mean you won't face challenges, but it ensures you're not facing them alone. This divine backup can give you the confidence to navigate even the most toxic environments with assurance and grace.

Dealing with Difficult Bosses: A Daniel Approach

Imagine navigating the tricky waters of workplace dynamics, especially when your boss seems to have taken a masterclass in making life challenging. Suppose we could all imitate Daniel from the Bible, who navigated his way through the lion's den of ancient Babylonian politics with grace and tact. In that case, we might find a way to deal with demanding bosses without losing our cool or compromising our values. Daniel's secret sauce? A blend of unwavering faith, impeccable conduct, and the wisdom to know when to stand firm and when to let his work do the talking.

Let's break down how Daniel maintained his integrity while dealing with some pretty high-stakes office politics. First, he never wavered from his commitment to his faith, even when it was anything but convenient. Remember the time he continued to pray openly despite knowing it could land him in a den of lions? That's the kind of commitment we're talking about. In today's context, this doesn't mean you should start a prayer meeting in the middle of your office if that's inappropriate, but it does mean you shouldn't hide your core values and beliefs. It's about integrating your faith into your work in a way that's respectful and true to who you are. For instance, if your boss demands that you do something against your ethical code, try respectfully declining and explaining your reasons with as much calm and dignity as possible.

Balancing respect for authority with assertiveness is like walking a tightrope. You want to show due respect to your boss's position, but not at the expense of your principles. So, how do you assert your beliefs without stepping on too many toes? It starts with respect—always approach your interactions with professionalism and courtesy. But when push comes to shove, assertiveness becomes your best friend. If a directive feels wrong to you, express your concerns respectfully. Use "I" statements to keep the conversation focused on your feelings and reactions rather than sounding accusatory. For example, saying, "I feel uncomfortable with this approach because it doesn't align with our company's stated ethics," presents your stance firmly yet politely.

Let prayer and seeking divine wisdom be your go-to strategies when dealing with difficult bosses. Before you respond to a challenging request or prepare for a potentially heated meeting, take some time to pray for wisdom and patience. Ask God to help you see the best way to handle the situation and for words that will speak truth and foster understanding. Sometimes, the solution may come to you in these quiet moments of seeking guidance or through the counsel of trusted family members or friends who can offer their perspectives and wisdom.

Building positive relationships with coworkers can also significantly ease the strain of working under a demanding boss. Think of your coworkers as your allies in the trenches. When you build strong, supportive relationships within your team, you create a mutual support network that can make the workplace more bearable for everyone. These alliances are about more than just having lunch buddies; they're about creating a supportive work environment where everyone feels valued and understood. Share your challenges and listen to theirs. Offer help when you can, and don't be afraid to ask for help when needed. Strong team dynamics can often buffer the negative impacts of a challenging boss, and sometimes, they can even influence the boss's behavior for the better.

Navigating the challenges of a demanding boss with a Daniel-like approach isn't about conquering or changing your boss—that's not in your power. It's about managing your actions and reactions to maintain your integrity, respect authority, and uphold your faith. It's about finding the courage to stand up for your beliefs, knowing when to pick your battles, and building alliances that foster a positive work environment. So next time you face a tough day at the office, remember Daniel. If he could handle jealous rivals and a lion's den with unwavering faith, there's hope for all of us, even in our workplaces. Keep your faith and integrity, and strive for excellence—your lion's den might turn into your place of triumph.

Creating Boundaries: A Nehemiah Strategy for Work

Imagine you're tasked with a massive project: rebuilding the walls of an entire city, much like Nehemiah in the good old Bible days. Now, translate that to modern times where your "city" is your personal workspace, and the "walls" are the boundaries you set to keep out the stressors and demands that threaten your peace and productivity. Nehemiah's story isn't just a tale of construction; it's a masterclass in setting and enforcing boundaries under pressure. Just as he faced opposition and distractions, you too might find yourself dealing with colleagues or tasks that infringe on your well-being. Learning from Nehemiah, you can discover the art of saying a firm yet polite "no" or "not now," ensuring your workday doesn't turn into a free-for-all where your priorities are trampled underfoot.

Setting professional boundaries is much like drawing a line in the sand. It's about making it clear to your coworkers and boss what you are willing to take on and what just doesn't fit into your work scope or schedule. This might mean saying no to last-minute requests requiring you to work late or declining to join yet another committee that meets during your supposed lunch break. It's crucial to communicate these boundaries clearly and assertively, without apology. Remember, setting boundaries isn't about being difficult but respecting your time and energy levels. Think of it as putting up a fence around your valuable garden of productivity and peace—without a gatekeeper, everything valuable inside is at risk of being trampled.

Dealing with opposition is part of the boundary-setting package. When Nehemiah was rebuilding Jerusalem's walls, he faced plenty of naysayers and enemies who tried to distract and discourage him. While you may not have literal enemies in the workplace, you'll likely encounter people who resist your boundaries, either because they're used to your constant availability or because they benefit from your willingness to overextend yourself. When opposition arises, keep your cool and reaffirm your boundaries with calm, reasoned explanations. If someone continues to push, it might be time to involve higher management or HR to help reinforce these limits. It's not about creating conflict; it's about maintaining a sustainable work environment where you can perform at your best.

Now, let's talk about maintaining a healthy work-life balance. It's easy to let work spill over into your personal life, especially when smartphones ping us with emails and messages at all hours. But here's where you need to be as firm as Nehemiah was with his wall-building strategy. Define precise cut-off times for work communication and stick to them as much as possible. This might mean turning off email notifications after a particular hour or chatting with your team about respecting personal time. Remember, your time outside work is precious—it's your opportunity to recharge, spend time with family, and engage in activities that refresh your spirit and body. Protecting this time is beneficial for you and your employer as well, as it prevents burnout and keeps you performing optimally.

Incorporating these strategies into your work life isn't just about making your days smoother; it's about setting a standard for respect and professionalism that can transform your workplace culture. By following Nehemiah's example, you not only rebuild the walls around your work "city" but also inspire those around you to respect and protect their own boundaries. This creates a work environment where everyone is empowered to contribute their best, free from unnecessary stress and chaos. So go ahead, set those boundaries with conviction, handle opposition with grace, and balance your work and personal life with the skill of a seasoned architect. Your peace of mind and productivity are worth it, and like Nehemiah's walls, the boundaries you build will stand firm, fostering a healthier, more respectful workplace.

Work as Worship: Maintaining Integrity in Toxic Situations

Think of your daily grind at work as more than a way to pay the bills. Imagine it as an offering, a sort of worship where every spreadsheet, every customer service call, and every packed lunch gulped at your desk becomes part of a more extensive, divine service to God. This notion may seem a stretch, especially on days when your boss is breathing down your neck about deadlines or when that one coworker never seems to have anything positive to say. Yet, embracing your work as an act of worship could transform how and why you work.

Viewing work as worship doesn't mean ignoring the realities of a challenging workplace. Instead, it invites a deeper perspective, where each challenge becomes a chance to demonstrate your faith through integrity and perseverance. When faced with ethical dilemmas or pressures to cut corners, consider what it means to work for the Lord and not for men (Colossians 3:23). It's about doing the right thing even when it's the hard thing, like choosing not to engage in gossip or standing up for a colleague who's being unfairly treated. These actions are your silent sermons; they preach integrity and character louder than words ever could.

Maintaining your integrity in a less-than-ideal work environment can feel like trying to stay clean while walking through a muddy field. It's messy and challenging; sometimes, each step forward sends splatters everywhere. But here's where your spiritual toolkit comes in handy. Arm yourself with prayer, a solid understanding of Biblical principles, and a commitment to live out those principles, come what may. Ask God for wisdom and clarity when unsure about the right course of action. Remember, being a witness for Jesus Christ isn't just about avoiding big ethical pitfalls; it's also about the smaller, everyday choices that shape how others see you and, more importantly, how they see Christ through you. The workplace provides an excellent stage to display your faith in Christ, often by actions alone, without even having to say anything. Many times, coworkers have asked me about my faith, not because I had talked about it, but because they saw how I lived daily. Since we may spend more time with our work team than with our own families, we might as well let the love and light of Jesus shine through us while we are there!

So allow God into your workplace. In seeking His guidance, you acknowledge that you're not alone. Whether it's a decision about a job offer, dealing with a tricky manager, or how to handle workplace conflict, inviting God into your career decisions brings a dimension of divine wisdom that can profoundly influence your career path. Make it a habit to seek His direction in all things, big and small. This ongoing dialogue with God about your work life helps you make better decisions and keeps you anchored to your true purpose and value in God's eyes, beyond titles and job descriptions.

Work, especially in a challenging environment, can sometimes feel like you're just surviving from paycheck to paycheck, from one weekend to the next. But when you shift your perspective to see your work as an act of worship, every task gains eternal significance, no matter how mundane. You're no longer just working for your boss or company but for the King of Kings. This shift doesn't change your circumstances but can transform your experience with them, filling your workdays with a greater sense of purpose and fulfillment.

As we wrap up this chapter, remember that your work is a form of worship, an opportunity to serve and glorify God through your daily tasks. By maintaining integrity, building spiritual resilience, and seeking divine guidance, you're not just surviving in your workplace but shining a light in it. These practices don't just make you a good team member at work; they make you a powerful witness to the grace and truth of the Gospel. So, as you move forward, carry these truths with you, and watch as they transform your work and your workplace witness. Be a godly example of the love of God, and you won't be stuck in a toxic work environment for long. God will bring new and better opportunities and promotions your way!

* * *

Reflection Questions:

Do I have any toxic coworkers? If so, who are they?

How can I show love to these people?

Is my work environment toxic?

What, if anything, can I do to make my workplace less toxic? (Examples: have a group meeting and share my thoughts, do random acts of kindness, change the atmosphere by being positive and uplifting, ask management to address the issue, etc.).

What steps can I take to find a new job? Can I start working on any special skills, degrees, or certifications to qualify for a better job with a better work environment?

Related Scriptures:

For promotion cometh neither from the east, nor from the west, Nor from the south. But God is the judge: He putteth down one, and setteth up another (Psalm 75:6-7, KJV).

Whatever you do, work at it with all your heart, as working for the Lord, not for human masters (Colossians 3:23, NIV).

Do not, therefore, fling away your fearless confidence, for it carries a great and glorious compensation of reward (Hebrews 10:35, AMPC).

Affirmations to Speak Aloud:
In the Name of Jesus, I declare:

- I am thankful for my job.
- I work at my job with all my heart, as if I am working for the Lord, not for man.
- I am a godly example at my job.

- I stand for Biblical principles even if I have to stand alone.
- God rewards my faithfulness by bringing me new and better job opportunities, bonuses, promotions, and raises.

* * *

Action Item(s):

Think of ways you can be a blessing to your coworkers (examples: buying them lunch, complimenting them, sharing their workload). Put these strategies into action. Who knows? Maybe it will open the door for you to share your faith in Christ with them.

CHAPTER 7

STRATEGIES FOR CONFRONTATION

So far, we have defined toxic relationships and looked at romance, family, friendships, and work examples. Now, let's suppose you have determined that you are in a toxic relationship, be it with a significant other, a relative, a friend, or a coworker, and it is time to confront the issue in order to have peace in your life. Congratulations on arriving at this realization! You have taken the first step to your freedom by defining the problem. We briefly looked at our next topic in the chapter on toxic friendships, but now, let's dive deeper into strategies to help with our most challenging step: confrontation.

Have you ever walked into a room and felt like you were about to face a dragon armed with a flimsy sword and a shield? Well, confronting toxic personalities can often feel that way. You know you must address the issue, but the thought alone can send you searching for the nearest exit. Don't worry, though—you're not headed into battle alone. This chapter is your guide to navigating the rocky terrains of confrontation with wisdom, strategy, and Biblical bravery, much like David did when he faced Goliath.

. . .

The David Approach: Facing Goliaths in Our Lives

Imagine standing in a valley, a giant looming over you, his shadow swallowing your courage. Sounds terrifying, right? But remember David, the young shepherd who faced Goliath not with fear but with unwavering faith. Your "Goliaths" might not be literal giants but toxic individuals who make your days challenging and your work environment or personal life miserable. The key here is not the size of the giant but the size of your faith. David didn't focus on Goliath's fearsome armor or towering height; he focused on God's power and the task before him. So, before you confront your modern-day Goliath, take a moment to remember why you're facing them: to restore peace, to stand up for justice, or to protect your well-being. Let your cause strengthen your resolve.

Confrontation doesn't mean charging in without a plan. That's the fast track to getting squashed by Goliath's big, metaphorical foot. Like David, who chose five smooth stones from the brook, pick your strategies carefully. Begin with prayer and even Biblical fasting. Seek God's guidance on when and how to confront the issue. Timing can be as crucial as the words you choose. Next, outline what you want to say. Keep your language clear and your goals realistic. To keep the person from getting defensive and disregarding everything you say, try focusing on "I" instead of "you" statements. For example, instead of saying, "You always disrespect me in front of other people," you could say, "I feel disrespected when you make jokes about me in front of other people." Or instead of saying, "You always insist on having everything your way on group projects," try saying, "I feel like my opinions are not valued when we are in a group setting." Phrasing is everything. Approach the situation with a humble, calm demeanor and a clear mind. Remember, the goal is not to escalate the conflict but to seek a resolution or make your stance known.

David had his sling; you have your strengths and talents. Maybe you're an excellent communicator who can articulate concerns with clarity and empathy. Or perhaps you're someone who radiates calm, able to defuse tensions with your serene presence. Empathy may come naturally to you if you can easily place yourself in another person's shoes. Whatever your strengths are, identify and use them as your tools to confront toxicity. These God-given talents are your slingshot, capable of delivering your message effectively and striking a chord. If you're unsure about your strengths, reflect on past conflicts where you handled things well. What skills did you use then? Those are the stones you'll load your sling with.

The most crucial part is trusting God's power to bring about victory. David's confidence was rooted in his faith, knowing that the battle ultimately belonged to God. When you step up to confront someone, carry that confidence with you. Believe that no matter the outcome, God uses the situation for your growth and His glory. Victory might not always mean winning the argument or changing the person's behavior; sometimes, it's about finding peace in standing up for yourself and aligning your actions with your values.

Setting Boundaries: What Would Jesus Do?

Imagine you're organizing your living room, a space meant for relaxation and comfort. Now, think of setting boundaries in toxic relationships similarly—it's about arranging your emotional and spiritual space so that it remains a safe and peaceful haven for you. In His time on earth, Jesus exemplified this beautifully. He didn't hesitate to carve out time for solitude to reconnect with His Father, even when crowds pressed in from all sides wanting more of His miraculous touch. He knew when to engage and when to withdraw, maintaining His well-being to fulfill His mission effectively. This wasn't Jesus being distant; it was Him being deliberate about His capacity and spiritual health. Let's unpack how to apply these principles to create healthy boundaries in your life.

Setting practical boundaries in toxic relationships might feel like building a fortress, but it's more about drawing a line in the sand. It begins with self-awareness. Identify what drains you emotionally and spiritually. Is it endless complaining, constant negativity, or disrespect for your time and efforts? Once you pinpoint these triggers, communicate them clearly. For example, if a friend constantly criticizes your faith or life choices, you might need to say, "I value our friendship, but I feel hurt when my beliefs are dismissed. Let's find other topics we can enjoy discussing." Remember, it's not about building walls but about laying down clear markers that protect your emotional and spiritual territory.

Moreover, showing love and compassion from a distance can be one of the most challenging undertakings in life. It's like watching someone you care about on the other side of a glass door—you can see them, you long to connect, but you know opening the door might let in a storm that could upheave your peaceful space. In toxic situations, especially those that threaten to pull you away from your faith or disrupt your peace, loving from a distance may be necessary. This might look like reducing the frequency of your interactions or choosing group settings over one-on-one meetups to lessen the intensity of the engagement. It's not about cutting people out of your life but about adjusting the proximity to protect your spiritual well-being.

Now, this is only possible with spiritual support. Just as Jesus often withdrew to pray, seeking strength and guidance from His Father, you, too, can find immense support through prayer and fellowship. Engage with your faith community—share your struggles and seek their prayers and wisdom. These interactions can be a lifeline, providing you with the encouragement and spiritual fortitude needed to maintain boundaries. Knowing others are praying for you can bolster your spirit more than expected.

Finally, remember that setting boundaries is a dynamic process. It evolves as your faith grows and your relationships shift and change. Regularly assess the health of your boundaries—ask yourself if they still serve the purpose of protecting and nurturing your spiritual growth. Adjustments might be necessary, and that's perfectly okay. It's all part of maintaining the health of your emotional and spiritual living room, ensuring it remains a place of peace and growth.

In this ongoing effort to protect your peace and cultivate a healthy spiritual environment, remember the grace with which Jesus navigated His relationships. He loved deeply and served humbly, yet he never lost sight of His mission and the boundaries that mission necessitated. Take heart from His example and be reassured that you can handle your relationships with the same grace and wisdom rooted in a deep and abiding faith.

Turning the Other Cheek: Misunderstandings Clarified

Have you ever been told to "turn the other cheek" and felt it implied you should stand there and take whatever is thrown your way with a smile? Well, let's clear the air. The concept often gets tossed around as a synonym for passivity, but let's dig into what it means and how it embodies strength rather than submission. When Jesus introduced this radical idea in Matthew 5:39, He wasn't advocating for a doormat lifestyle. Instead, He taught us the power of controlled, intentional responses that disarm aggressors and preserve our dignity.

Think about it this way: turning the other cheek isn't about letting someone repeatedly hurt you. It's about choosing not to escalate the situation, thereby maintaining control over your reactions. It's a form of strength that says, "I have the power to choose my response, and I choose peace." This approach doesn't just apply to physical confrontations—it's relevant in verbal clashes, too. In toxic situations, especially where words can sometimes hit harder than fists, mastering the art of a composed response can be your most excellent shield. It allows you to respond to hostility, not with retaliation, which can perpetuate the cycle of aggression, but with a demeanor that diffuses tension.

Now, let's talk about the fine line between assertiveness and aggression. Being assertive means you respect yourself enough to express your feelings and needs honestly and respectfully. Aggression, on the other hand, involves asserting your feelings and beliefs in a way that violates the rights of others. It's the difference between saying, "I feel upset when you speak to me in that tone. Can we please keep our discussion respectful?" versus, "Stop talking to me like that or else!" See the difference? One opens the door for constructive communication; the other slams it shut, possibly hitting someone in the nose in the process.

Jesus, in His interactions, gave us some prime examples of assertive behavior that never crossed into aggression. Did He lash out when the Pharisees tried to trap Him with tricky questions? Nope. He answered wisely, staying true to His mission and maintaining His composure, all while standing firm in His message. His responses were not passive; they were full of wisdom, designed to make His point without stooping to His opponents' level of deceit and manipulation. Jesus' assertiveness was like a well-aimed arrow, hitting the mark every time but never intending to kill.

Responding righteously rather than reactively in toxic situations means taking a breath before you react. It's about asking yourself, "Is my response going to reflect my faith and values, or am I just reacting out of hurt or anger?" This pause, this moment of reflection, can be the difference between a response that mends relationships and one that tears them further apart. It's about embodying the fruits of the Spirit—love, joy, peace, patience, kindness, goodness, faithfulness, gentleness, and self-control—even in the heat of conflict.

When you choose to respond in a way that aligns with these virtues, you're not just turning the other cheek in the traditional sense; you're actively choosing to engage in a way that promotes reconciliation and understanding. This doesn't guarantee that every conflict will be resolved perfectly, but it does ensure that you're part of the solution, not the problem. It keeps the doors of communication open and protects your inner peace, preventing the toxicity from seeping deeper into your life.

In mastering this art of righteous response, draw strength from your faith in Christ. Remember, each time you choose to respond with grace rather than aggression, you're not just keeping the peace; you're standing as a witness to the transformative power of your beliefs. So, the next time you face a situation that tempts you to react in the heat of the moment, take a deep breath, remember Jesus' example, and choose a response that reflects your strength, faith, and commitment to living out the Gospel. This is how you turn the other cheek—not with passivity, but with powerful, purposeful peace.

As you approach the confrontation of toxic individuals in your life, remember this powerful passage from Ephesians: "For we wrestle not against flesh and blood, but against principalities, against powers, against the rulers of the darkness of this world, against spiritual wickedness in high places" (Ephesians 6:10-12). As much as the toxic individual may have hurt you, they really don't even realize the depths of their harm. The enemy wants nothing more than to make you hate this person and to remove you from your love walk. Why? Faith worketh by love (Galatians 5:7). We need faith for everything in life: faith for God to protect us from harm, faith for our car to get us to work and back, faith that what we eat won't poison us, faith for our children to be safe at school, faith to achieve our dreams and goals, and the list goes on and on.

The key to successfully operating in this faith is to walk in love. When we hate someone (perhaps justifiably so!), we are not walking in love. That's why satan uses people to torment us so that we will not walk in love. In turn, our faith will not work, and we will not fulfill God's dreams, goals, and plans for our lives.

So, the battle is so much bigger than the toxic person in front of us. It's a spiritual war between good and evil, light and darkness, faith and fear. The toxic individual has no idea they are being used by satan to get us out of our love walk. This does not excuse their behavior, but it helps us forgive and heal when we realize they don't know what they are doing. It's not the person we are fighting; it's satan. And the best news, my friend, is that Jesus has already won that fight for us!

So rely on Him as you confront the toxic individuals in your life. Speak the truth in love. Be clear and concise. State your feelings plainly without being accusatory. Give the person time to change. Pray that they will be sensitive to the convicting voice of the Holy Spirit in their heart. After doing all this, if the toxic individual still refuses to change, seek God's will to determine if it's time for you to move on, knowing you have done everything in your power to mend the relationship, and your hands can be clean before God. I am praying for you, my friend! Confrontation is not easy, but please know that you are not alone. God Almighty loves you deeply; He sees every tear you cry and is waiting for you to seek solace in His Presence as you walk this difficult but courageous road to freedom.

* * *

Reflection Questions:

Is there a toxic individual in my life that I need to confront? If so, who?

How can I frame my conversation with this person to focus on my feelings and hurt rather than on accusing them of their wrongdoing?

* * *

Related Scriptures:

For in Jesus Christ neither circumcision availeth any thing, nor uncircumcision; but faith which worketh by love (Galatians 5:6, KJV).

...speaking the truth in love, we will grow to become in every respect the mature body of Him Who is the head, that is, Christ (Ephesians 4:15, NIV).

Let your conversation be always full of grace, seasoned with salt, so that you may know how to answer everyone (Colossians 4:6, NIV).

And be not grieved and depressed, for the joy of the Lord is your strength and stronghold (Nehemiah 8:10, AMPC).

* * *

Affirmations to Speak Aloud:
In the Name of Jesus, I declare:

- I am a peaceful person.
- I am a joy to be around.
- I am a blessing to everyone I meet.
- I am consistently joyful.

- I do everything within my power to live at peace with everyone.
- When toxic individuals refuse to change, I forgive them and move on, for I wrestle not against flesh and blood.

Action Item(s):

As you prepare to confront toxic people in your life, spend time in prayer and fasting. Enter the conversation fully confident and at peace. Stay calm, focus on your feelings, and use "I" statements rather than solely accusing them of wrongdoing.

CHAPTER 8

HEALING AND FORGIVENESS

So far, we have defined toxic relationships and how they may manifest in romance, friendships, family, and work. We've also looked at how to confront toxic individuals. But how about after you've taken all the right steps and you still feel hurt and broken? In this chapter, let's tackle these issues together as we explore healing and forgiveness so you can begin your life of hope and freedom.

Have you ever felt like you were holding onto a hot coal, waiting to throw it at someone? That's how resentment works—and trust me, it burns us far more than anyone else. Forgiveness is like dropping that coal; it's about healing the burns and not setting yourself on fire in the process. This chapter isn't just about saying "I forgive you" and moving on. It's about understanding how deep the roots of forgiveness go and how they can heal your heart and potentially transform your whole life. Let's dive into this topic together!

The Healing Power of Forgiveness: A Biblical Blueprint

Forgiveness isn't just a nice thing that good people should do; it's a core element of living a full and healthy life. It's like cleaning out a wound; painful, yes, but necessary for proper healing. When you hold onto grudges, it's like allowing that wound to fester—harmful not just to your mental health but also to your spiritual wellness. The act of forgiving can release you from a cycle of pain and bitterness, freeing up space in your heart for peace and joy to grow. Forgiveness isn't about excusing what they did; it's about setting yourself free.

Now, if we're talking role models for forgiveness, no one tops the charts like God Himself. Through Jesus Christ's sacrifice, God offered forgiveness for all our wrongdoings—knowing full well that we might mess up again (and again). His example isn't about ignoring the wrong or pretending it didn't hurt. It's about choosing to love and heal rather than to hold onto the pain. This divine model of forgiveness shows us the power of unconditional love and sets a high bar—loving others not because they always deserve it but because love is the very essence of who God is.

Understanding forgiveness as a process is crucial. It's rarely a one-and-done deal. Think of it as layers of an onion—sometimes you think you've gotten to the core, only to find there's more to peel back. It can involve acknowledging the hurt, feeling the emotions, choosing to forgive, and then possibly choosing it all over again when old feelings bubble up. It's normal, and it's okay. Each layer peeled back is a step towards deeper healing.

But as we discussed in Chapter 2, forgiveness doesn't always mean reconciliation. It's possible—and sometimes necessary—to forgive someone while also choosing not to restore the relationship to what it once was. This can be the case when trust has been deeply broken, or ongoing harm occurs. Forgiveness in such cases means you let go of the bitterness and wish them well, but you may choose to love and pray for them from a distance. It's about protecting your peace and healing without exposing yourself to further harm.

As we explore forgiveness, remember it's not about weakening your boundaries or pretending the hurt never happened. It's about healing from those hurts so thoroughly that they no longer control you. It's about freeing up your heart to fully give and receive love. So, let's keep peeling back those layers, one forgiving step at a time. Your heart will thank you for it, and your life might just change in ways you never expected.

Protecting Yourself Post-Forgiveness

Let's talk about a tricky topic: forgiving and forgetting. Forgetting doesn't mean we have totally lost all memory of a situation; it means we remember it differently. We remember it from the perspective of how God brought us through the situation and what we learned from it to guide us in similar future experiences. This isn't about keeping a mental list of wrongs or brewing over past hurts. It's about wisely using your past experiences as guardrails for your future. Think of it like keeping a recipe you know was a hit at the last family gathering. You keep the recipe not because you want to dwell on that particular dinner but because it helps you recreate the success next time. Similarly, remembering the patterns or behaviors that led to hurt can help you recognize them before you're too deep in a situation that might hurt you again. This kind of memory is protective, not punitive.

Now, maintaining boundaries post-forgiveness is crucial. It's like having a safety net while walking that tightrope. Just because you've forgiven someone doesn't mean you have to return to how things were. Maybe you decide that certain topics are off-limits in conversations, or you choose to meet in group settings rather than one-on-one. These boundaries aren't signs of unforgiveness; they are your way of protecting your emotional and spiritual well-being. It's okay to adjust the closeness of your relationships based on past experiences to protect your peace. It's not about building walls but installing safety rails that keep everyone on solid ground.

Learning from betrayal can feel like sifting through the debris after a storm. It's messy, and honestly, who wants to poke around in wreckage? However, just as you might learn not to park under an old tree during a storm, you can learn from past relational storms to avoid future damage. Start by looking for patterns. Do you tend to trust too quickly? Are there red flags you've ignored? Understanding these patterns isn't about beating yourself up but equipping yourself with knowledge. This self-awareness can be incredibly empowering because it turns painful experiences into lessons that sharpen your discernment and decision-making.

Seeking God's wisdom in navigating these post-forgiveness relationships is like finding a lighthouse in the fog. It keeps you from crashing into the rocks. When unsure how to set or maintain boundaries or process the memories of past hurts, turn to God in prayer. Ask for the wisdom to handle each situation in a way that honors Him and preserves your dignity. Scriptures like James 1:5, which promises that God gives wisdom generously to all without finding fault, can be incredibly comforting. It's a reminder that you don't have to figure this out alone. God is ready to guide you through every step, helping you to genuinely forgive while safe-guarding your heart with wisdom.

Navigating the complexities of forgiveness and memory requires a delicate balance. It's about walking in freedom from bitterness while guarding against future hurt. It's perfectly okay to move forward with an open heart and a wise mind, using your past not as a weapon but as a blueprint for building healthier, more fulfilling relationships. As you continue to navigate these waters, remember that each step taken in wisdom and love brings you closer to the peace and joy that forgiveness promises.

. . .

Self-Forgiveness: Overcoming Guilt

Let's face it: who among us hasn't been the star of their own personal blame game show at some point? You know, that mental marathon where you replay every decision, word, action, and reaction and somehow end up as the villain in your own story. It's exhausting and, let's be honest, not exactly a self-esteem booster. Self-forgiveness is about stepping off this endless loop. It's about recognizing that carrying guilt and shame around is like lugging a giant backpack full of rocks—it slows you down and wears you out. Instead, imagine setting that bag down and walking freely. Sounds liberating, right?

First, identifying self-blame can be trickier than finding a quiet room at a family reunion. It often masquerades as justifiable self-criticism. "I shouldn't have trusted them" or "I always mess things up" are common tunes we play in our heads. Recognizing these patterns is the first step toward silencing that harsh inner critic. The reality is that blaming yourself for all the toxicity in relationships is like blaming yourself for the rain—neither is under your control. Relationships are a two-way street, and toxicity is never a solo act. Acknowledging this can be incredibly freeing and is the first step in the journey of self-forgiveness.

Now, let's chat about God's grace—a vast, profound, yet intimately personal concept. Understanding God's grace in the context of self-forgiveness means recognizing that God doesn't keep a tally of our wrongs. His grace doesn't come in limited editions or run out after multiple uses. It's like an ever-flowing stream, constantly available to cleanse, renew, and refresh our spirits. Embracing this truth can radically change how you view yourself and your mistakes. It's the ultimate assurance that even when you falter, you are still valued, loved, and worthy of forgiveness. This divine acceptance is your cue to extend the same grace to yourself.

Moving on to practical steps for self-forgiveness, imagine you're learning to ride a bike. You wouldn't expect to nail it on your first go, right? There will be wobbles and falls—it's part of the process. Similarly, self-forgiveness is a process. Start small. Forgive yourself for one thing each day. It could be as simple as forgiving yourself for not doing the dishes. The key is consistency. Over time, this daily practice builds your 'forgiveness muscles,' making it easier to handle the bigger stuff. Another practical step is to write forgiveness letters to yourself. Detail what you forgive yourself for and why. These letters can be powerful reminders of your humanity and your growth.

Lastly, releasing shame and fully embracing your identity in Christ is akin to shedding an old, ill-fitting coat in favor of one that suits you perfectly. Shame often tells us that our worth is conditional, based on what we do or how others perceive us. However, in Christ, we find an identity that is not based on these shifting sands but on solid ground. This identity says you are created in the image of God, redeemed, and loved unconditionally. Embracing this truth can transform self-perception from perpetual striving and failing to living out the joyful reality of being God's beloved. Strategies to reinforce this include surrounding yourself with truth—scriptures that affirm your identity in Christ, books and sermons that reinforce this truth, and a community that reminds you of it consistently.

As we wrap up this exploration of forgiveness, remember that forgiveness doesn't excuse toxic behavior; it sets *you* free! Don't forget to rely on God for strength to forgive others and yourself. You are not to blame if a relationship has turned toxic, but you can take the first step to healing and restoration. Remember to pray for the toxic individual that they will also find the freedom and solace you have found in Christ.

* * *

Reflection Questions:

Who do I need to forgive?

Do I need to forgive myself of anything? Or am I blaming myself for the toxicity?

* * *

Related Scriptures:

It is for freedom that Christ has set us free. Stand firm, then, and do not let yourselves be burdened again by a yoke of slavery (Galatians 5:1, NIV).

You, my brothers and sisters, were called to be free. But do not use your freedom to indulge the flesh; rather, serve one another (Galatians 5:13, NIV).

Now the Lord is the Spirit, and where the Spirit of the Lord is, there is freedom (2 Corinthians 3:17, NIV).

Then you will know the truth, and the truth will set you free (John 8:32, NIV).

* * *

Affirmations to Speak Aloud:
In the Name of Jesus, I declare:

- I am forgiven.

- I receive God's love and forgiveness.
- I forgive freely.
- I radiate the love of Christ everywhere I go.
- Other people see Jesus in me.

Action Item(s):

If you have identified someone you need to forgive, write their name at the top of your prayer list and commit to praying for them daily. Remember, when you choose to forgive, you may not feel any differently at first. Forgiveness is a process; it may take time. Take the step of forgiveness, and the feelings will eventually follow.

CHAPTER 9

EMPOWERING YOURSELF TO BREAK THE CYCLE

Well, my friend, we have reached the final chapter! We have come a long way together on our journey to deciphering toxic relationships. We defined toxic relationships in romance, friendships, family, and work. We examined strategies for confronting toxic individuals and how to recover and heal after the relationships change or end. Now, let's look to the future by examining ways to empower ourselves to break the cycle of toxicity.

Rediscovering Your Worth in Christ After Toxicity

Imagine you are at a bustling flea market, rummaging through piles of 'once-loved' and 'barely-touched' treasures. Amidst the chaos, you stumble upon a gorgeous vintage mirror with an ornately carved frame. You pick it up, dust it off, and briefly catch a glimpse of your reflection. But it's not just you in the reflection; it's a vision of who you are in Christ—priceless, cherished, and deeply loved. This mirror doesn't show you a distorted image shaped by past toxic relationships but reflects your true worth.

99

This chapter is much like finding that mirror. It's about wiping away the dust left by others' damaging words and actions to reveal the radiant reflection of your inherent worth in Christ.

Think of it as a diamond—sure, it can get smudged or buried in the mud, but does that change its value? Absolutely not! Your worth, embedded in the fact that you are wonderfully made by God (Psalm 139:14), remains untouched, no matter how others have treated you. It's not a variable dependent on someone's mood or whims; it's a constant, as unchangeable as God's love for you. Toxic relationships might have made you feel like you're worth less, especially if you were constantly criticized or undermined. But here's the good news: the opinions or treatments of others do not define your true value. You are invaluable not because of what you can do, who you know, or what you have achieved but simply because you are God's creation.

Now, let's tackle a more challenging topic—overcoming shame. It's like an unwanted sticker on your favorite book; it's pesky and leaves a residue if not properly removed. Shame, especially from toxic relationships, can make you feel unworthy of love, success, or happiness. It whispers lies into the deepest parts of your soul. But here's how you can counter it: by understanding that God's view of you is not based on your past, your mistakes, or how others have seen you. Romans 8:1 tells us, "Therefore, there is now no condemnation for those who are in Christ Jesus." No condemnation. That means the shame you feel does not come from God. Peel off that sticker of shame by saturating your mind with the truth of God's Word and embracing the forgiveness and freedom offered through Christ.

Speak aloud the affirmations and Scriptures included at the end of each chapter of this book. Claim them for your life. Believe that God wrote them about you and just for you. Use the Word of God like medicine; apply it to all your hurts and heartaches. The amazing news is you cannot overdose on God's Word, so speak it over yourself as many times and as often as you need until it gets down in your soul, rooting out the lies of the enemy. Renew your mind to God's Word, which means flushing out anything contrary to the Word and only allowing the Word to occupy your mind. This is why speaking affirmations aloud is so important; you can't say one thing and think another. You can't say, "I am made in the image of God and have great worth," while you're thinking you're a loser.

Keep in mind this isn't about a one-time detox; it's about a daily commitment to replace toxic thoughts with life-giving truths. Romans 12:2 urges us not to conform to the pattern of this world but to be transformed by the renewing of our minds. This transformation happens as you immerse yourself in Scripture, spend time in prayer, and surround yourself with positive, faith-affirming influences. Maybe you don't know any faith-filled individuals, or you're unable to be around them often. That's okay. You can listen to Word-saturated preachers and teachers who can impart truths in you that took them their entire lives to discover. It's like updating the old software in your brain; the more you renew your mind with God's truths, the less room there is for toxic residue to linger.

By embracing your inherent worth, using Scriptural affirmations, shedding the burden of shame, and continually renewing your mind to God's Word, you're not just surviving past toxic influences but thriving beyond them. You're rediscovering the masterpiece that you are—a priceless reflection of God's love, designed for purpose and filled with potential. So, keep polishing that mirror of self-perception with the truth, and let your true worth shine for the world to see.

As you grow in your relationship with God through Christ, you will be okay with being alone if needed. You will not compromise your standards or beliefs to rush into a romantic relationship or join the crowd. You will realize that it is okay not to fit in with everyone else because there is far greater joy in fulfilling God's plan for your life. You will realize you are never truly alone because He is always with you, sticking closer than a brother. Furthermore, I stand as a living testimony that when you are willing to wait forever for God-ordained relationships, you won't have to wait long. As you seek Jesus as your first Love, He will also provide other loving relationships for you. So seek first His kingdom and His righteousness, and all else will be added to you (Matthew 6:33).

Recognizing Your Patterns: The First Step to Change

Once you realize and accept your inherent value in Christ, you may find yourself longing to start new relationships, be they romantic, friendship, or others. Remember to always keep Jesus at the center of each new interaction. Before you embark on this journey, knowing when you are ready is essential. Some practical ways to determine if you are ready for new relationships include self-reflection, recognizing common patterns, considering Biblical insights, and taking action to break the cycle of toxicity.

Self-reflection is like having a heart-to-heart with your most honest friend. It doesn't always tell you what you want to hear, but it always tells you what you need to know. Recognizing the patterns that lead you into toxic relationships is about taking a long, hard look in the mirror and being honest with what you see. Maybe you tend to value others' opinions over your own, or perhaps you find yourself drawn to relationships where you feel needed because it boosts your sense of worth. Whatever those patterns are, identifying them is like mapping the landmines in a field—you'll know exactly where not to step as you move forward.

Let's look at some common patterns that might sound familiar. First up is the 'rescuer' role. If you find yourself drawn to partners you can 'fix,' you might be walking this line. Then there's the 'people pleaser' pattern, where saying 'no' feels like you're breaking the law. Low self-esteem can also lead you down a path where any attention feels like good attention, even when it's not. And let's not forget the fear of loneliness, which can make any company seem better than no company, pushing you to hold onto relationships long past their expiration date.

It may be hard to come to terms with the root of your relationship issues, but the sooner you find the root, the sooner you can prune it out and flourish without it. If you are a 'rescuer,' remind yourself that you cannot change anyone. Leave the changing up to God and pray for the person from a distance until they get their act together. Do not enter a relationship with a spiritual fixer-upper, someone who is not mature in their walk with Christ.

If you're a 'people pleaser,' tell yourself it is okay if not everyone likes you. That's life. Sometimes, people just don't like you, and that's okay. They may dislike you even if you do everything you can to please them. Accept it and move on. You are better off without them dragging you down.

We have already determined how to improve self-esteem by focusing on our inherent worth in Christ. Flee from anyone who puts you down; it's not worth starting a relationship with such a toxic individual. If you determine your self-esteem is plummeting whenever you're around a specific individual, take the hard step to end the relationship.

Finally, when you feel lonely, lean into godly relationships, such as church groups and Bible study partners. Ask God to bring healthy relationships into your life. Do not tolerate a toxic person in your life just because you feel lonely.

Determine to never repeat the same toxic relationship patterns. Ask God for clarity and strength to avoid such situations and a way of escape if you find yourself in one. Flee any relationship that throws up red flags as soon as you spot the warning signs. Remember, Christ has set you free from your past, and you are not to blame for any wrong treatment directed toward you. However, now that you have identified the cycle of toxicity and found your worth in Christ, you know better than to willingly enter another toxic relationship. You are to blame if you purposely ignore the warning signs.

Taking Control of Your Relationship Destiny

Remember you have been given the power to choose new relationships going forward. This power of choice is your steering wheel in the journey of relationships. Take control of the direction in which your relationships are moving. Recognize that you can steer toward healthier, more fulfilling relationships no matter the patterns or past disappointments.

This might mean setting stronger boundaries, spending more time with those who uplift you, or even stepping away from relationships that feel like constant uphill battles. We can't change others, but we can adjust our own settings to better align with what brings us peace and fulfillment.

Diving deeper, let's reflect on the beautiful gift of free will, a divine endowment from God that allows you to make choices that align with your values and aspirations. It's like being given a blank canvas and a set of vibrant colors to create a piece of artwork. The strokes you decide to paint—bold, subtle, or somewhere in between—are entirely up to you. In relationships, this means actively choosing people who respect and enrich your life and encourage you to expand in love, faith, and joy rather than confine you to the shadows of doubt and insecurity.

Now, how do we make these empowered choices? First, by setting standards. This isn't about crafting an unrealistic checklist for relationships but defining what core values are non-negotiable for you. Is it kindness? Integrity? A shared faith? Think of these standards as your relationship code, guiding you in whom you allow into your life's inner circle. Next is knowing your worth, which is crucial. You are a treasure, profoundly loved by God, deserving of respect and love. When you truly embrace this, your choices shift dramatically—you start to attract and choose relationships that mirror this intrinsic value rather than contradict it.

Scriptures offer abundant encouragement and guidance. Proverbs 3:6 reminds us, "In all your ways acknowledge Him, and He will make straight your paths." When you bring God into your relationship decisions, seeking His wisdom and guidance, your paths are straightened and illuminated. Take time to consult God on who you allow into your life, asking for discernment and strength to make good, not just convenient choices. This divine collaboration ensures that your relationship choices are not random picks in the dark but deliberate selections that lead to growth and blessings.

Creating a Life You Love: Write the Vision and Set Goals

Imagine standing at the end of your life looking back on all the years. What would you like to see? This is what writing the vision is all about—envisioning the life you truly want to lead, one that resonates with your soul and aligns with your values. Crafting this vision isn't just daydreaming; it's an artful and intentional practice that sets the stage for your future, particularly in cultivating fulfilling relationships and a profound sense of purpose.

Writing the vision is also Biblical. Habakkuk 2:2 says, "Write the vision, and make it plain." So take some time to dream. Get a dream notebook and write down your dreams for your future. In doing so, you are writing your vision for your life. Obviously, don't write down bad things or anything that doesn't align with the Word of God. But get your dreams down on paper and review them regularly. While you're at it, have some fun and create your own vision board on which you display pictures that correspond with your dreams. I suggest checking out Terri Savelle Foy's teachings on vision boards, which have totally changed my life and can do the same for you. What you focus on, you become. As you dwell on your vision for fulfilling relationships, you will start attracting them. God will bring people into your life that align with the God-given dreams He has given you.

Start by asking yourself, "What does a fulfilling life look like for me?" Is it nurturing a family, building a career that impacts lives, traveling the world, or perhaps a beautiful blend of all three? Picture yourself waking up on a perfect day, fully immersed in activities that fill you with joy and purpose. Who's with you? What are you doing? How do you feel? These aren't just idle questions; they're powerful introspections that draw the blueprint of your life. Envisioning a life you love sets a hopeful trajectory, guiding your decisions and helping you focus on what truly matters.

Integrating your faith brings a deeper dimension to your aspirations when setting goals, anchoring them in personal ambition and divine purpose. It's like consulting the Master Builder on your building plans—ensuring that each goal fits your desires and aligns with the greater good He has planned for you. This might mean setting goals that fulfill you and serve others—like volunteering in your community, starting a faith-based project, or even enhancing your relationships in ways that reflect Christ's love. When your goals are set with faith, they are infused with perseverance and significance, making them resilient to life's ebb and flow.

Now, create an action plan for achieving these goals. Remember, goals should be SMART: specific, measurable, achievable, relevant, and time-bound. Take the first step to reaching your goals, no matter how small it may be. Every step forward, however tiny, is a victory. Celebrate it!

Did you have that tough conversation with a friend to clear the air? Treat yourself to a manicure. Did you complete a week of devotions without skipping? Share that joy with your accountability partner. Did you finally break up with that lazy boyfriend who doesn't want to work? Girl, buy yourself something nice!

Celebrating progress is more than giving yourself a pat on the back; it reinforces positive behaviors that get you closer to your ultimate vision. It reminds you that every step is bringing you more in line with God's will for your life.

As you close this chapter, take a moment to appreciate how far you have come. You're not just surviving; you're intentionally crafting a life brimming with joy, purpose, and love. This proactive stance elevates your existence and transforms you into a beacon of hope and inspiration for others. So, keep dreaming, planning, and achieving. God has empowered you to break free from toxic relationships, end the cycle of toxicity, and live the life you have envisioned. Go for it!

Reflection Questions:

What patterns do I see in my relationships? Am I a rescuer, a people pleaser, someone with low self-esteem, or do I fear being alone?

What actions can I take to break these cycles?

What qualities do I desire in future relationships (romantic, friendship, family, work)?

Related Scriptures:

I am my beloved's, and my beloved is mine (Song of Solomon 6:3, KJV).

Be ye are a chosen generation, a royal priesthood, an holy nation, a peculiar people; that ye should shew forth the praises of Him Who hath called you out of darkness into His marvelous light (1 Peter 2:9, KJV).

The Lord thy God in the midst of thee is mighty; He will save; He will rejoice over thee with joy; He will rest in His love; He will joy over thee with singing (Zephaniah 3:17, KJV).

* * *

Affirmations to Speak Aloud:
I declare in the Name of Jesus:

- I am loved by God.
- I am worthy of love.
- I attract godly relationships.
- I do not enter into toxic relationships.
- God rejoices over me with joy.
- I rest in His love because He is more than enough.
- God rejoices over me with singing.
- I am living the life God ordained for me to live.
- I am fulfilling the dreams and goals He has placed inside of me.
- I am fulfilling my God-given assignment on this Earth.

* * *

Action Item(s):
Take a moment to reflect on the patterns you've recognized in

your relationships. Write down at least one pattern you want to change and a specific action you plan to take this week to alter your usual response. This small step today can be the giant leap toward healthier, more fulfilling relationships tomorrow. Remember, every incredible journey begins with a decision to walk a different path—even if it's in fabulous shoes!

CONCLUSION

Well, my friend, we've traveled together through the tangled vines of toxic relationships, and look how far we've come! From the romantic entanglements that left us dizzy to the family ties that felt more like knots, friendships that turned out to be mirages, and work environments that tested our endurance. Together, we've navigated these tricky waters, guided by the timeless wisdom of the Bible, the therapeutic power of journaling, and a steadfast faith in God's plan for a life free from such entanglements.

We've armed ourselves with critical strategies:

- Learning to spot the red flags of toxicity
- Drawing the line with healthy boundaries
- Taking action to confront and break the cycle of toxicity
- Leaning on God's Word and our faith community

These tools aren't just lifelines but the building blocks for the healthier relationships we all deserve.

Remember, your worth is immeasurable, and no amount of toxicity can change that. Embrace the boundaries you've set—they're not barriers but bridges to a more peaceful life. Let your relationship with God deepen, for in His love, there is transformative healing. And let's not forget the strength we draw from our communities, our circles of support that bolster us in times of need.

As you stand now, perhaps you can feel the shift within—a move from a place of pain to a place of power, where hope replaces despair and renewal washes over past hurts. You've likely noticed how your relationship view has matured, now painted with strokes of mutual respect, genuine love, and unwavering faith.

Keep those journal questions, Bible verses, positive affirmations, and action items close to your heart. They are your continuous companions in reflection, helping you to keep in tune with yourself, your relationships, and your faith.

Now, let's talk action—continue to nurture your freedom and growth. Engage actively with support groups, seek counseling if you feel the waves of past toxins wash ashore, and deepen your relationship with God. Share your journey; your story could be the beacon of hope for someone else navigating their stormy seas.

You are a treasure, wonderfully made and destined for greatness beyond the shadows of toxicity. With each step forward, remember that you are equipped with an indomitable spirit and a heart capable of immense love and resilience.

So, what are you waiting for? Let today be the day you step fully into the sunlight, leaving the shadows behind. Embrace a future where your relationships are marked by health, respect, and divine love.

And now, let me offer a prayer for your path ahead:

Heavenly Father, I ask for Your loving guidance and protection as my dear reader takes the lessons from these pages into their heart and life. Grant them strength to face any challenge, wisdom to choose paths that lead to peace, and comfort in knowing they never walk alone. May their life be filled with Your grace, their relationships flourish under Your care, and their spirit be effervescent with the joy of Your everlasting love. Amen.

Go forth, emboldened and renewed, for your journey continues, blessed and beautiful, under His watchful eyes. Here's to healthier relationships, profound healing, and a joy-filled life!

Did you enjoy this book?

Please take a quick minute to let other people know how great it is!

Scan the QR code to post your review now! Thanks a million!

REFERENCES

- New International Version Bible. (2011). Zondervan.
- Amplified Classic Bible. (1987). Zondervan.
- King James Version Bible. (1769/1987). Cambridge University Press.
- 21 important Bible verses about choosing friends. (n.d.). Bible Reasons. https://biblereasons.com/choosing-friends/
- Paul's inspired teachings on marriage. (n.d.). BYU Religious Studies Center. https://rsc.byu.edu/go-ye-all-world/pauls-inspired-teachings-marriage
- Jesus set boundaries. (n.d.). Soul Shepherding. https://www.soulshepherding.org/jesus-set-boundaries/
- 21 best Psalms for comfort & hope. (2020, June 8). Psalm 91. https://psalm91.com/2020/06/08/21-best-psalms-for-comfort-hope-for-the-hurting-overwhelmed-and-grieving/
- 7 ways to improve communication in relationships. (n.d.). Positive Psychology. https://positivepsychology.com/communication-in-relationships/
- Seven biblical steps to resolving conflict. (n.d.). Pastors.com. https://blog.pastors.com/articles/seven-biblical-steps-to-resolving-conflict/
- 17 manipulation tactics abusers use. (2023, July 20). Choosing Therapy. https://www.choosingtherapy.com/manipulation-tactics/
- Five essential boundaries in the workplace. (2023, November 1). Psychology Today. https://www.psychologytoday.com/us/blog/living-better-with-boundaries/202311/five-types-of-essential-workplace-boundaries
- How to leave an abusive relationship safely. (2023, May 24). Verywell Mind. https://www.verywellmind.com/making-a-safety-plan-to-escape-abusive-relationship-5069959
- 13 wisdom principles when ending a dating relationship: How to break up to the glory of God. (2014, August 26). Biblical Counseling Coalition. https://www.biblicalcounselingcoalition.org/2014/08/26/13-wisdom-principles-when-ending-a-dating-relationship-how-to-break-up-to-the-glory-of-god/
- Gaslight (1944). (n.d.). IMDb. https://www.imdb.com/title/tt0036855/

- How to heal from a toxic relationship. (n.d.). Growing Self. https://www.growingself.com/leaving-toxic-relationship/
- How to deal with toxic family members biblically (7 steps). (n.d.). Equipping Godly Women. https://equippinggodlywomen.com/community/reader-question-respond-toxic-family-members/
- Falk, E. B., & Berkman, E. T. (2016). Self-affirmation activates brain systems associated with … National Institutes of Health (NIH). https://www.ncbi.nlm.nih.gov/pmc/articles/PMC4814782/
- The top Bible verses about forgiving yourself in scripture. (n.d.). Bible Study Tools. https://www.biblestudytools.com/topical-verses/bible-verses-about-forgiving-yourself/
- Let it burn: The four stages of true forgiveness. (n.d.). Conscious. https://conscious.is/blogs/let-it-burn-the-four-stages-of-true-forgiveness
- Healing from identity loss after narcissistic abuse. (2018, August 3). PsychCentral. https://psychcentral.com/blog/liberation/2018/08/healing-from-identity-loss-after-narcissistic-abuse
- Setting healthy boundaries in relationships. (n.d.). HelpGuide. https://www.helpguide.org/articles/relationships-communication/setting-healthy-boundaries-in-relationships.htm
- What does the Bible say about setting personal boundaries? (2019, November 22). Treasured Ministries. https://treasuredministries.com/blog/2019/11/22/what-does-the-bible-say-about-setting-personal-boundarie/
- 20 women's stories on how they learned to set boundaries. (2021, January 19). Medium. https://medium.com/@NikkiElizDemere/20-womens-stories-on-how-they-learned-to-set-boundaries-8889a5235c60
- Benefits of self-compassion: 7 benefits and how to practice. (n.d.). PsychCentral. https://psychcentral.com/blog/practicing-self-compassion-when-you-have-a-mental-illness
- How solo travel can change your life. (n.d.). Under30Experiences. https://www.under30experiences.com/blog/how-solo-travel-can-change-your-life
- The role of faith in overcoming adversity. (n.d.). FasterCapital. https://fastercapital.com/topics/the-role-of-faith-in-overcoming-adversity.html
- Narrative therapy for trauma: How telling your story can heal. (n.d.).

Healthline. https://www.healthline.com/health/mental-health/narrative-therapy-for-trauma

- Four biblical signs of healthy relationships. (n.d.). IBL Ministry. https://www.iblministry.org/blog/four-biblical-signs-of-healthy-relationships
- Learning to trust after an abusive relationship. (2022, April 6). Psychology Today. https://www.psychologytoday.com/us/blog/invisible-bruises/202204/learning-to-trust-after-an-abusive-relationship
- 13 red flags in relationships. (n.d.). Verywell Mind. https://www.verywellmind.com/10-red-flags-in-relationships-5194592
- 5 ways to establish good communication early on in your relationship. (n.d.). Zoosk. https://www.zoosk.com/date-mix/relationship-advice/establish-good-communication-early/
- The power of emotional check-ins: How they can improve your mental health and well-being. (n.d.). Be Strong. https://bestrongmh.com/blog/the-power-of-emotional-check-ins-how-they-can-improve-your-mental-health-and-well-being
- Exercise for mental health. (2004, September). National Institutes of Health (NIH). https://www.ncbi.nlm.nih.gov/pmc/articles/PMC1470658/
- Efficacy of journaling in the management of mental illness. (2022, March 22). National Institutes of Health (NIH). https://www.ncbi.nlm.nih.gov/pmc/articles/PMC8935176/
- Controlled comparison of family cognitive behavioral therapy. (2011, September). National Institutes of Health (NIH). https://www.ncbi.nlm.nih.gov/pmc/articles/PMC3205429/
- Benefits of peer support groups in the treatment of addiction. (2016, October). National Institutes of Health (NIH). https://www.ncbi.nlm.nih.gov/pmc/articles/PMC5047716/
- Online support groups vs. in-person meetings. (n.d.). American Addiction Centers. https://americanaddictioncenters.org/blog/online-support-groups
- How the church can support emotional health. (2014, February). Christianity Today. https://www.christianitytoday.com/women-leaders/2014/february/how-church-can-support-emotional-health.html
- Building your support network. (2021, December). Everymind.

https://everymindatwork.com/wp-content/uploads/2021/12/
Building-Your-Support-Network.pdf

- The healing power of EMDR. (n.d.). Scottsdale Providence Recovery Center. https://scottsdaleprovidence.com/emdr/
- Mindfulness and emotion regulation: Insights from ... (2016, February). National Institutes of Health (NIH). https://www.ncbi.nlm.nih.gov/pmc/articles/PMC5337506/
- 10 tips for setting boundaries online. (n.d.). PsychCentral. https://psychcentral.com/lib/10-tips-for-setting-boundaries-online
- 28 uplifting Bible verses about adversity (with commentary). (n.d.). Marisa D'Amore. https://marisadamore.com/verses/28-uplifting-bible-verses-about-adversity
- How to write SMART goals (with examples). (2023, February). Atlassian. https://www.atlassian.com/blog/productivity/how-to-write-smart-goals
- 7 stories of hope in the Bible when times are hard. (n.d.). Love Fast Live Slow. https://lovefastliveslow.com/7-stories-of-hope-in-the-bible-when-times-are-hard/
- Why celebrating addiction recovery milestones is important. (n.d.). Bold Health. https://boldhealthinc.com/celebrating-addiction-recovery-milestones/
- The power of testimony: Sharing your faith story with others. (2020, September). iBelieve. https://www.ibelieve.com/christian-living/the-power-of-testimony-sharing-your-faith-story-with-others.html

ABOUT THE AUTHOR

Mary Melissa Hall grew up in the beautiful Appalachian Mountains of North Georgia. She now lives in sunny South Carolina with her husband and three children. As an educator for over a decade, she is passionate about seeking wisdom and continuously improving her life and the lives of those around her. She considers it her greatest endeavor to know Jesus and make Him known.